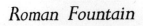

Roman Fountain

MICHELANGELO:
Study for a
figure in 'The
Last Judgment'.
(*Venice Academy*)

Roman
Fountain

by

Hugh Walpole

LONDON
MACMILLAN & CO. LTD
1940

COPYRIGHT

PRINTED IN GREAT BRITAIN
BY R. & R. CLARK, LIMITED, EDINBURGH

THIS BOOK
IS FOR
HAROLD CHEEVERS

FRONTISPIECE

It's no use raising a shout.
No, Honey, you can cut that right out.
I don't want any more hugs;
Make me some fresh tea, fetch me some rugs.
Here am I, here are you:
But what does it mean?   What are we going to do?

W. H. AUDEN

I   70,193

IT was on Monday, February 13th, 1939, and the
day before the burial of Pope Pius XI that I was
flung into Rome again. ' Flung ' is the right
word, for on the Saturday evening I was sitting in
the town-hall of Keswick listening to my friends
as they performed that very simple play *The Passing of the Third Floor Back*; an old lady crept up
to me and whispered that I was wanted at the
telephone.

So, just outside, even as I caught the squab-
blings of the very unlikely lodgers in Mr. Jerome's
play, I heard my Agent's voice: " The Pope's
funeral is being hastened. It is to be Monday
night. The only way you can get there in time is
to fly. You will have to fly by Berlin."

Roman Fountain

I detest flying. I didn't want to go to Germany. I had to motor all through the night to London. Why did I do these hateful things?

To report the Pope's funeral and subsequent events for an International Press Syndicate would be interesting. But that wasn't enough. Just then I was extremely happy writing about Father Campion's execution in my grand Elizabethan novel. It had rained for a fortnight without stopping, but when you are working rain is a gift from God. You have no urge to climb the hill. You stick to your business.

If, indeed, the Pope were to be buried in any other town but Rome — in New York, say, or Vienna or Berlin — I would not go. Go! I would not even consider going.

I had liked the idea of this Pope, Pius XI, whereas of most Popes I have been sublimely unaware. Pius XI had a most pleasant countenance. He was strong of body. He had climbed some mountain in the Alps that no one had climbed before. And, of late, he had stood firmly against the enemies of his religion. Yes — but did I want to see him buried?

Not enough to leave my grand Elizabethan novel in which I believe so passionately and *shall* believe — until the last word is written!

Roman Fountain

To leave your characters with their legs in the air! There is nothing more discourteous! One of my two heroes, Robin Herries, is on his way now, at 11.5 A.M. Roman time, February 16th, 1939, to witness Campion's execution. The rain is pouring down, the gullies are alive with running mud; smelling and rude people jostle him at every step. What a situation in which to leave him! No one but I can liberate him. And yet it is likely that he will be standing in the rain for two whole months yet, when I had thought to liberate him before the sun had set, before my evening meal comes on a tray while I am listening to Honegger's *King David* from Queen's Hall, and my friend and companion is laying out the chessmen so that a game may be begun the moment that Honegger has finished. . . . So Robin Herries *should* have been allowed his comfort.

As it is I am miserable when I think of him, and last night when, in the crimson and crystal Roman Opera House, I listened to *Salome* (does anyone know why *all* the musical women in Rome talk throughout every opera?), at the very moment when they raised the grid above Jokanaan and bid him come forth, I was thinking of Robin and of Campion and of my relation Henry Walpole who,

3

on that melancholy day, was spattered by Campion's blood and was converted thereby.

Yes, it would have taken more than the Pope's funeral to force me to leave Robin Herries and the Keswick rain; to leave also the bank of snow-drops and the first three crocuses, about which flowers I have no intention of saying pretty things. But the fact is that when I return to Brackenburn after the new Pope's Coronation they will be gone.

On the other hand for a fortnight now we have been making a rockery, turning a stream that runs from the top of Catbells and planting roughly stones and rocks, pulled by an ancient farm-horse and Frank the gardener out of the wood below my house and above the Lake. At this moment the rockery is very ugly. A little baby earthquake has thrown the stones about my garden, and there they lie, sullenly refusing to be anything but unnatural.

And yet I know, when I return in April, my rockery will seem as permanent as the Bowder Stone. It could not have been that there was ever a garden without a rockery. . . . But enough. Whatever else may occur I must not be lyrical about gardens. I have too much feeling and too little knowledge — unlike Mr. Evelyn who had so much knowledge and no feeling at all. The best writer about gardens in our time remains still ' Elizabeth ' — whose genius I have the greatest pleasure here in saluting. And why do I say she has genius? Because no one else has been able to perform her especial little step in the universal Ballet. No. Not Mrs. E—— . . . and most certainly not Mr. B——. If you doubt me read that very blessed book *Fräulein Schmidt and Mr. Anstruther* and then, if I am still challenged, read *Elizabeth in Rügen*.

And so to return. I left for Rome not because of the Pope's funeral or because of the money that I would get for recording it, but because I wanted to find a lost Fountain.

Don't think that I intend at this point to become mystical or fantastic. Not at all. I am severely practical and as realistic as Proust when he describes the lift-boy at the Grand Hotel at Balbec. Nor do I mention Balbec in order to show you that I have read all the best writers and know them intimately, but simply because the lift-boy at Balbec is very real to me and so, before I have done, I would like my lost Roman Fountain to be to you.

To explain about this Fountain I must go back a very long way — all the way back to 1909 when

Roman Fountain

I published my first novel and did all the reviewing on the morning *Standard*. I was happy then — but not so happy as I am now. I wasn't so happy then because I was so fiercely ambitious.

I had had such luck. Smith, Elder published *The Wooden Horse*; Mr. Jeyes — whose name be for ever blessed — had engaged me on the *Standard* at £150 a year; Robert Ross had given a luncheon for me to which he invited H. G. Wells, Max Beerbohm, Clutton - Brock, Harold Nicolson (he said to Harold: " Lunch with me to meet a new young genius." How sarcastically Harold told me that years later, and I expect Robert said it sarcastically too!) Best of all Henry James was befriending me. All this within a year! But of course I was off my head and thought that genius was the right word for me — the only time, before or since, that I ever did.

But this isn't an autobiography. No, no. It will be twenty years before I write one. This at the moment is to explain how I went to Rome for the first time all those years ago.

I suddenly decided one afternoon to go. An American friend of mine was off on business to Switzerland and Venice. Venice! Oh no! Venice? I had never been to Italy. Would I come that very night? Yes, I would. And before that evening I was given a letter that Henry James wrote to his old lady friend who lived in the old Venetian Palace that comes into *The Wings of the Dove* — or is it *The Golden Bowl*? Perhaps it comes into both.

But this isn't now about my American friend or Switzerland or Venice, where I was sick with happiness — yes, actually sick in a room above a shop hung with strings of onions and the green-blue water lapping its feet — sick in that very room that had a ' Pietà ' on the rough mottled wall and they said it was Sienese School, but I can remember to this very day that old crushed rose colour and the white thin feet of the Christ. Sick just after I had been introduced to Horatio Brown, who didn't mind, but said it was shell-fish probably and not happiness.

He was exceedingly kind and advised me to make my permanent home in Venice. He said Venice would make me the kind of writer I'd like to be. Would it? I have never been the writer I'd like to be — not austere, nor with a style like a well-built house, no cracks, no paper in the broken windows, no mice eating the cheese. I'd like to be a writer with Addison's prose, Dickens' vitality, Montaigne's realism, Proust's apprehension, Hardy's first-hand creativeness. So here

7

Roman Fountain

I am — all alone by myself and writing as best I can and enjoying it most of the time.

But what about Rome? I went on there from Venice. Three days I had there. I slept in a hotel by the station. When I saw the Colosseum for the first time, I'll swear there was a lion poking out its brown anxious face near the urinal, but there were no Christians. No one but myself, the lion and the urinal attendant.

I did a lot of sight-seeing in those three days. I was ravished with delight, except for the Vatican Museum where the white blobs of clay puritanically clumped on as fig-leaves spoilt all the beauty. I lay on my back in the Sistine Chapel and looked through the glass the guide gave me. I bought a coloured reproduction of *Adam and Eve*, with the serpent twined round the tree exactly like Bernini's pillars in St. Peter's. I was drunk with wonder and sharp-tasting Chianti, discovered by me for the first time here.

However — what about the Fountain?

I discovered the Trevi on my very first dark evening, and threw a penny into it. I was told to do this by a book that I still have: *Rome in Three Days*.

My other books were Zola's *Rome*, George Moore's *Esther Waters*, *Paradise Lost* and Wilkie

Collins' *Armadale*. I read *Paradise Lost* right through from beginning to end on this happy journey. Why I brought it with me I can't think. Snobbery, I suspect, to impress my American friend. I had read only little pieces of it before. Now I couldn't stop. Yes. I read it through from end to end. And have linked it in my mind with the Colosseum ever since.

There are many delightful things I would care to say about *Paradise Lost*, but who would care to read them? ' Hugh Walpole on *Paradise Lost*.' No, no; it would never do. ' Aldous Huxley on *Paradise Lost* — Virginia Woolf on *Paradise Lost* ', everyone will rush to read.

Why would no one be interested in me on *Paradise Lost*? — for I have really some delightful things to say.

Only a week or two ago at luncheon Ethel Sands said : " You would be, I am sure, a very bad critic." (' Would be ' was hard. Didn't she know that I did a page of literary criticism in a newspaper every week of my life?) She added kindly: " Because you are creative." But that was only a friendly sop.

No, why is it I would not myself even read ' Hugh Walpole on *Paradise Lost* ' while Virginia, whose *Common Reader* is before me at this moment . . .

I feel, as Tonks says he felt, before these intellects as a rustic before his Squire.

But that is not truly so. I admire my brain.
I see it quite clearly as a comfortably-bodied,
bright-eyed animal with a frisky tail and soft
strong paws. It goes everywhere and can eat
practically anything. It is handsome, rare and
strong. What does it lack? I don't know and I
don't want anyone to tell me. I just know that
no one wants to hear anything I have to say about
Paradise Lost — and that is that.

I shall never tell anyone what I think about
Paradise Lost except that I look back and see Satan,
contemplating this planet before he makes his
descent. How handsome, sad and evil he is!

And so exactly was Chaliapin in the Norodney
Dom in Petrograd, in the Brocken scene of Boito's
Mefistofele — stark naked, brooding, on the top of
the hill . . .

But to return to my Fountain.

. . . . . .

. . . . . .

. . . . . .

One afternoon of March 1909, I came upon
this Fountain in Rome.

It was my second day in Rome. What can I
recall of the surrounding circumstances?

II

I KNOW that the afternoon was warm, but the
Romans thought it cold, for they were all wearing
overcoats. I was the only young man in the whole
of Rome on that day *not* wearing an overcoat.
Sometimes you would see quite an old Roman
with grizzled cheeks, grizzled moustaches, grizzled
coat, his shirt open at the neck. No overcoat.
He wasn't cold!

I was still in a state to be astonished by the
flowers. Nowhere out of Italy do you see them
banked up into a kind of pyramid of lovely freshness as you do in Italy, and especially in Rome —
but of course everyone knows about flowers in
Rome. Why be naïvely excited at this late day?
Except that I *was* naïf then, and I *was* excited, and

I wanted to buy and buy and buy. . . . Two kinds of things I wanted to buy — flowers and the little bronze copies of the classical statues — the Faun, the Boy with the Water-Bottle, the Narcissus, the Venus.

But I had no money, or very, very little. I had to watch every lira. I had my return ticket in my pocket-book so that I knew that I should see England again. But that was about all.

I did buy, however, a pot of lilies of the valley. I had never seen lilies of the valley in a pot before and I felt as though I had been given an especial prize. I gave the pot, when I left, to the black-haired, brown-faced, big-stomached rascal who cleaned my room in the little hotel near the station. I know he was a rascal, for he stole my silver cigarette-case—my cigarette-case that some friends of mine had given me at Cambridge on my twenty-first birthday. He was a rascal and also I was afraid of him. I have been afraid of only four people in my life since I have grown up : this Italian rascal, Katherine Mansfield, Rebecca West, and — a friend of mine.

Of Katherine Mansfield I was so desperately afraid that I trembled at the sound of her voice. This happened almost directly after my return to

Roman Fountain

England from this first visit to Rome. In 1910 Mansfield and Murry had a paper called *Rhythm*, and I contributed. We had meetings in Murry's room (he and she were known as The Tigers in those days). Besides Mansfield and Murry there were D. H. Lawrence, Gaudier-Breszka, J. D. Beresford, Gilbert Cannan. These were the Highbrows of that day.

I wanted to be a Highbrow but didn't know how to be one. So I went in agitation to these gatherings, and there was Lawrence, his long thin legs expressing contemptuous energy (but he was charming in those days — soft and gentle and feeling very little of the ' dark urge ' that obsessed him in later years). And there was Katherine Mansfield with her black bang of hair and eyes like gimlets. It was entirely my own fault that I was frightened. She didn't want me to be. But whenever she spoke to me I said the most idiotic things, answering questions with such foolishness that there was embarrassment in the room. No one wanted to be unkind. The trouble was that I wanted to be clever and of course Mansfield saw through me — at once, long before I spoke.

Of Rebecca West I have long ceased to be afraid. She is kind and friendly. There remains,

then, only one person in the world now of whom
I, fifty-five years of age, am afraid. *He* frightens
me because he makes me suspicious of my own
honesty, my own kindliness of heart, my own
sincerity. I am honest, kind, sincere, just, like
my fellows — that is, at this moment and at that.
We are all capable of amazing kindliness, wonderful sincerity. The right moments, the noble
feelings, they come and they go.

But my friend makes me, when I meet him,
wonder whether I am *ever* sincere, ever kind —
whether there is not a base and mean motive
behind all my actions. And so, although I like
and admire him, I am afraid of him and meet him
as seldom as may be.

I gave the Italian at the hotel the pot of
lilies of the valley because I was afraid of him,
because I knew that my farewell tip was too small
and because I was sure that he had stolen my
cigarette-case. We hunted for it together and
he patted me on the back because I had lost it.

On this especial day it was warm and I had
luncheon in a little restaurant in a side street not
far from that huge and hideous white and gold
monstrosity, the Victor Emmanuel monument.

It was in this little restaurant that I met Mr.

Montmorency, and it was he who showed me the Fountain.

I pushed the door and entered from the sunlight into the dark, and blinked. Then my sight cleared and I saw it was a very simple place, with large water-bottles on the tables, sand on the floor and a picture of the King of Italy on the wall. The half-dozen little tables were occupied and I hesitated before I sat down all alone at the big table that glittered with water-bottles and rather unfriendly emptiness.

I heard then an English ' almost Oxford ' voice behind me say : " There is room here."

I turned round blushing, for I felt that I must look so *very* English for a stranger to be so *very* sure of my nationality simply by glancing at me. There sat Mr. Montmorency, wiping his mouth very carefully after his soup. He was, I saw at once, on the seedy side. He was stout and short and the top of his head was bald except for one lock of greasy hair pasted like seaweed on the shining surface. His round fat face had been shaved yesterday perhaps but certainly not today, the cuffs of his shirt were frayed, his soft collar was grey so that you must not say that it was dirty. His finger-nails were also grey. He had a soft wet mouth, a pudgy nose, but his eyes were touching, asking for kindliness, but restless with insecurity. All this I did not, perhaps, notice at once, but I sat down quite eagerly beside him because I thought it kind of him to invite me.

I wore in those days very ridiculous pince-nez that perched on the end of my nose and were attached by a little chain to my waistcoat. This attachment was a wheel that, often unexpectedly, would give a whirl, absorbing the chain and dragging the pince-nez from my nose. They flew off now and, with my own shining wondering eyes, I gazed on Mr. Montmorency. My gaze made him uncomfortable; his eyes almost disappeared and he lifted one pudgy soiled hand and said, " Two is company . . ."

(I am recovering all this as I write. I have not thought of Mr. Montmorency for many many years, but now he is with me in this room. I can hear every word. I need to invent nothing at all. He is at my very elbow prompting me, for, now that he is a ghost, it is the truth only that he cares about.)

" Now — what are you going to eat? Let me advise you."

But I knew what I was going to eat. *Spaghetti al Burro* (I had discovered already that any kind of sauce with it, whether meat or tomato, was for me a crime) and *Vitello*. Oh, *Vitello*, *Vitello*, *Vitello*, how constant, how inevitable are you in Italy! How many millions of little calves there must be pressing about the butcher, offering their innocent throats! But I didn't know that. Roman veal seemed to me a miracle of succulent cheapness, another wonder in a wonderful land.

Mr. Montmorency appeared disappointed at my simpleness. He said something about *fritto misto al mare* and *scampi*. I hadn't the least idea what these were, but, when he explained, I told him that I didn't want fish.

" When you are sight-seeing all day," I said, " you need meat."

His eloquent eyes sparkled.

" Ah, you are new to Rome? "

" I have never been here before."

" You are staying long? "

I sighed. " Tomorrow is my last day."

" How long have you been here? "

" I have only three days in all."

At once then he took charge of me. I was, I suppose, exactly what he was needing.

" What have you seen? "

" St. Peter's, the Vatican Museum, the Forum, the Colosseum," I answered proudly. It seemed a lot in such a very short time. " And whatever happens I must see Keats' grave."

" Ah, Keats." His whole body sighed. " There was a poet. ' One whose name was writ in water.' You care for poetry? "

" More than anything else in the world — except music. Oh yes, and painting of course."

" The Arts. You are yourself an artist? "

" I am a writer — a novelist and a critic."

He enquired further.

" One novel of mine has been published, another shortly will be. I do all the reviewing on the *Standard* newspaper."

It was a splendid record. I didn't mind in the least that the whole world should know it. That, in all probability, I should find on my return to England that I was a reviewer no longer, because of this little unpermitted holiday, had not as yet occurred to me.

Mr. Montmorency laid his pudgy hand on my arm.

" I too am a writer," he said softly, and producing from his pocket a very shabby pocket-book he laid before me a little collection of dirty dog-eared cuttings.

Politely I examined them and read that the *East Lothian Herald* considered in 1903 that Mr. Montmorency's *Lilac and Violet* was ' a volume of

mellifluous verse, agreeable to the ear and wholesome in tone ', and that the *Wiltshire Journal* held
that ' Mr. Robert Montmorency shows promise in
many of these pleasant verses ', and that the *Hull
Observer* considered that ' this little volume cannot
fail to please '.

" You are a poet? " I said appreciatively.

" I *was* a poet," he answered with a deep bitter-
ness, " but one cannot live on poetry — no —
unless one truckles to a base public. That too
Keats found — yes, and many another."

Hurriedly he collected the cuttings as though
he feared lest I should steal them, and replaced
them in his pocket.

" You live in Rome? " I asked him.

" Live! Yes — if you can call it living."

I could see that he already considered me his
private personal property. I didn't mind that in
the least. I was, I was sure, well able to keep my
independence and I felt for him a warm patronizing superiority. I was filled with an eager
benevolence towards the whole world. *I loved
every dog and wished that every dog should love me*
— a motto from Jean Paul Richter that I had
already placed on the first page of my first novel.

Some of my superiority, I must confess, immediately after this deserted me; for I was sadly

embarrassed by my spaghetti. Alone I managed
not too badly, but now I wished to show that eating
spaghetti was a very old game to me, and so in my
eagerness and attempted assurance I made a sad
mess of it.

Mr. Montmorency showed me what I ought to
do, but my pince-nez behaved just then like the
very devil. I was the more uncomfortable too
because I had an odd feeling that Mr. Montmorency
wanted himself to eat my spaghetti. He stared at
it with a real and hungry longing.

I had ordered a bottle of red Chianti and to
my surprise saw that this was already half finished.
Then I saw that Mr. Montmorency had been helping himself with friendly liberality. I had by now,
hunger having conquered shyness, all but finished
my plate of spaghetti. There was still some more
in the dish, and the waiter moved forward to fill
my plate again. But I waved my hand with the
over-fed lazy patronage of a Tiberius. ' Enough is
as good as a feast.'

" If you don't want it —— " said Mr. Montmorency.

His eyes glistened — with greed, with affection, with gratitude? And in any case he had been
drinking my Chianti.

" Another bottle," I said resplendently, for I

had learnt by now that Chianti is very cheap
in Italy.

" My friend "— Mr. Montmorency's voice quiv-
ered — " this is one of the first happy moments
I have had for weeks."

I was a little drunk myself and I beamed bene-
ficently. I was drunk really with happiness rather
than with Chianti. To be sitting in this kindly,
genial Rome in a restaurant with sand on the floor,
and with all these great monuments of Time
on every side of me. And there was another
reason for happiness of which I will speak in a
moment. I know that I am touching danger here.
It is wrong to be happy and to be happy for such
very insufficient reasons. I will be platitudinous.
I will say that one man is happy and another is
not for reasons far apart from virtue or vice,
worldly success or failure, possessions or lack
of them — even from considerations of good
health or bad.

Happiness comes, I know, from some spring
within a man — from some curious *adjustment* to
life. The happiest people I have known in this
world have been the Saints — and, after these, the
men and women who get immediate and conscious
enjoyment from little things. I know that great
physical pain, long continued, can override this

happiness, for five years ago I experienced that, and I believe that the loss of some loved person can change the body and colour of life so completely that it is not a question of happiness or unhappiness any more, but a business of discipline and control.

My own happiness has come so clearly from three things — my consciousness of enjoyment at the time I experience it, and enjoyment especially of the Arts; my work; and my friends — that I am naturally inclined to suppose that others too get their happiness from these sources. But often they do not. One man I know is happy only when he is playing bridge, but as he plays bridge morning, noon and night he is always happy. A woman I know has no friends, but she loves clothes and, as she is rich, she can change her dresses four times a day — and does. She is a very happy woman.

I am sure that it is this question of adjustment to conditions that brings happiness, but in my own case it is to this day — and will be until I die — a matter of surprise, constant and unfailing, that I have the fun I do, see and hear the lovely things I do, enjoy the friendships I do. It is as though I expect to wake up at any moment and find this all a dream, to wake up and discover that I am back in the dormitory at R———, with the sudden sleep-awakened terror of immediate pain, pain spiritual, pain mental, pain physical. So do not envy me my happiness. Somewhere, once, it was otherwise. . . .

My desire that everyone else should be happy makes me often sentimental. But I do not think that I see this cruel and remorseless world falsely. With my personal belief that this world is a place for soul-training, I do not see how this life could be other than the extraordinary mixture of terror and splendour that it is. After all, in actual experience it is, I suppose, a matter of choice. 'You pay your money . . .'

One of my greatest friends, a man whom I admire and love, is exactly the opposite from me in this. He is, by reason of his temperament, bound to choose 'thumbs down' rather than 'thumbs up'. He has had everything that man can desire — fantastic success, a delightful wife, charming children. But things are never as they might be. Something always spoils the picture.

I would be intensely irritating to him (sometimes I am) were it not that my optimism seems to him so childish, so foolish, that he has developed an almost paternal feeling for me, although in years he is much my junior.

" Poor old Hugh!   He has never grown up and never will."

I don't resent this at all.   I like it.   If I met myself somewhere I should feel, in all probability, like that *about* myself!

III

THE boy who, in 1909, talked to Mr. Montmorency did not question his happiness at all or think it wrong that he should be happy.

Until the age of twenty he had been nearly always unhappy, had had no friends, had been constantly misunderstood. So at least he felt, not at all realizing that it had been his own fault that people had disliked him — because he was dislikeable. (The good and excellent reason why people *are* disliked.) He was now only twenty-five years of age so that he had had little time as yet to be happy.

And I had, as I have already said, another reason for happiness that morning. On my way I had hung for a long long time outside a small rather dusty-windowed shop, much as small boys stand outside sweet-shops with their noses pressed to the window. This little shop displayed bronze replicas of some of the famous bronzes — all the familiar ones were there: certainly the Faun, the Boy with the Thorn, the Narcissus, the Michael Angelo David. One or two of the larger ones were priced. Too high, too high, alas, for my powers! There were also little bronzes, especially of the Faun and the Narcissus, but they were so cheaply made as to be almost boneless and featureless.

I hung there, on suspended desire, panting! When I want something that seems to me beautiful I do not just want it. I want it with a desire that is hunger and thirst and lechery and longing to be good all in one!

Should I run all the risks and buy one of the larger bronzes? "After all," said the tempter, "you have your return fare to London. Tomorrow you need have but one meal. You know that you will be able to pay your hotel bill. It is true that you must eat very little in the train on your return journey, but that will do you no harm. A little starvation, a little martyrdom of the body — how excellent for you! Moreover, within three days from now this suffering will be forgotten. You will remember none of it, or if you do remember it, it will be with pride. And you will have the statue — the Faun, the David, the Narcissus — whichever you prefer. You will have it for ever. It will be on your writing-table, its beauty, its strength, its symmetry ever before you. And how much better you will write because of its presence!

"You cannot obtain such bronzes in London save at an impossible price. It will be long before you return to Rome, although you did throw your penny into the Trevi Fountain. Come! Purchase! Purchase! Hasn't some great man said somewhere that the only acquisitions in his life that he regretted were those he hadn't made! Think how, in a week's time, you will be regretting your lost opportunity! There, seated in your Chelsea room with your copper coal-scuttle, your coloured print on the wall of Botticelli's *Venus*, your set of Walter Pater that you won as an Essay Prize at Cambridge, your vase of cut glass that will be holding, in all probability, daffodils — think how these, your beloved possessions, now so intimately connected with you, so rightly proud of their friendship with you — think how they will gently reproach you for refusing to add to their number one whom they would so gladly welcome. And see! The Narcissus has raised his head, his uplifted finger admonishes you. He is eager to leave his dusty window and become your friend and learn the English language and make the acquaintance of Walter Pater! Can you resist him? *Ought* you to resist him?"

This did not seem to me a kind of Barrie-whimsy at the time, and for one very good reason: because we did not, in 1909, consider Barrie the worse for his whimsy — not, that is, when he was at his best. *The Admirable Crichton* we considered one of the best comedies in English, cynical, if anything — whimsical not at all.

For another, I remember quite clearly that the Narcissus did seem to me, in my then excited state of imagination, to make a personal appeal. The little statue was in that grey-green bronze proper to its Naples original and was then (catching light from its original) as it is now, one of the loveliest things on earth.

My hand was on the door of the shop — I was almost inside it — when I saw that the shop was closed. A little notice hung there from which, although I knew no Italian, I rightly understood that the proprietor was away until three. I was saved then — saved and defeated, for I walked away, hanging my head, feeling that I was leaving behind me a Narcissus affronted, insulted, deserted.

Roman Fountain

And then, only two steps further and I was facing a window filled with postcards, maps, guides, bottles of ink, coils of string, and pen-holders. The postcards were of the kind to which I was already accustomed — views of Rome, the Palatine, the Colosseum, the Pantheon, the Trevi Fountain, St. Peter's — but beside them was something that made my eyes dilate: a page of rough drawings on what seemed to be faded yellow paper, a page of drawings labelled *Disegni dei Grandi Maestri — Sanzio Raffaelo* and priced three lire!

I knew of course at once that these could not be the original drawings. Young and foolish though I was, I yet knew enough for that! Not the originals, but how close to them? Could anyone save an expert tell the difference? Well, yes, perhaps anybody could.

But, in all essentials, they were the same.

It was at that moment, standing in front of that little shop, that I realized the great truth that fragments from a Master's workshop have often more of the Master in them than the finished works themselves. It seemed to me that I could trace the hand of Raphael, careless, prodigal, in every line. It was as though he himself had stepped forward to me and said: " There, young man, if

29

you want it, take it. I am only too glad." And
three lire! Three lire! That I could afford. This
could and should be mine and I would still be rich,
still have three meals on the train and a good full
day in Rome tomorrow.

I entered the shop. The fine woman with
jet-black hair so dark that it seemed to have
purple shadows in it, a plump sallow countenance,
dark hair on the upper lip, a firm massive bosom,
a black dress that had the sombre dinginess of a
Pirandello widow (although I knew of course
nothing at all of Pirandello at that time) — this
Roman lady is close to me now, at my very elbow.
For, in that dark little shop, smelling of glue and
pasta, I tasted to the full of the Rome that I
had really expected to find, the Rome that until
now had never offered me a glimpse of its melodramatic presence.

The Rome that I had *expected* to find was the
Rome of three persons, a Rome of literature and
uninhibited romance, a Rome, as I shall presently
explain, empty of all details, composed of atmosphere, of one or two speechless figures as full of
fate as the Statue of the Commander.

The three writers who had given me this Rome
were Nathaniel Hawthorne, J. H. Shorthouse and
Francis Marion Crawford. Of Hawthorne's *Trans-*

formation I will say little at this point. The *story* of *Transformation* had always seemed to me, even when I first read it at the age of twelve or thereabouts, extremely silly, and it seems to me extremely silly still. But *Transformation* had been my spiritual guide-book to Rome — not that I absorbed from it, with any accuracy, interesting details.

Inaccurate I have always been and will always be. My mind floats in a kind of summer mist. All objects are veiled, but by a beautiful, shimmering sun. I think also that to be hazy about detail has the happy effect of making detail for ever new — nothing is old or stale on the tenth beholding when the nine preceding it have been radiantly myopic. In any case what I got from Hawthorne was a place of sun and heat, of fountains and pines, of flowers and ancient ruins. Yes, and of dark figures moving in and out of the savage Colosseum, the lovely Palatine, the high Janiculum. Murder was never far away, and the thunder-clouds stealthily invaded the sun.

Nor will I say much here of *John Inglesant*, for that has its later place; save that here also I commingled Rome with sin and resolved revenge. But of Francis Marion Crawford — how base and ungrateful I would be not to pay him my tribute

31

whenever, on turning a corner, his altar, neglected now, the stone chipped, the homely bunch of flowers faded, the very letters of the name obscured, comes into view!

After the great Names have been named — Homer, Sophocles, Aeschylus, Dante, Shakespeare, Milton, Goethe — how uncertain, how subject to every turn and twist of the current of fashion, taste, world affairs, individual experiences, are all the others in the mighty stream of literature! What has any writer to do but fulfil the creative impulse within him, stronger than any other impulse? Indeed he cannot help himself, and will know no greater joy, wherever his life will take him, than that supreme moment when, suspended in air, he can look down on the creative impulse, just satisfied, and believe for a brief instant that the created work is good!

For how brief an instant! But, because of that, he is, however loudly he may protest and curse his fate and abuse his fellow-man, one of the most fortunate of mortals! After that the rest is, for the most part, silence. And yet, not altogether so. Kipling, in his autobiography, tells us that he was creatively strengthened by a romance by Walter Besant — *All in a Garden Fair*. It is to that work that he pays his tribute, and a pretty poor book it is too. The history of no published book is ever ended. An awful truth, but for every author, cherishing his works of creation as fathers cherish their plainer children, a consoling one.

It may be that the romances of Francis Marion Crawford will never be read again, although I fancy that the future historian may find his ' Risorgimento ' Roman novels — *Saracinesca*, *Sant' Ilario*, *Don Orsino*, *Corleone* — so interesting and fruitful a record of a place and a period that he will forgive their stiffness, their triteness, their platitudes, their simple figures of good and bad morality.

But now — what am I about? Am I already betraying ingratitude? I am not. An artist lives by his faults as well as his virtues. He lives by anything at all that gives him personality and makes him, however slight his stature, someone apart from all other men.

There will never be a Francis Marion Crawford again. His very naïveté prevents it. And yet was it naïveté? He had precisely the standards that Joseph Conrad had after him. He believed in fidelity, courage, the honourable word, patriotism, love between masculine men and feminine women. His men indeed were so very masculine, his women so very feminine, that you

33

feel it to be remarkable, as you read, that they ever found a common ground. Perhaps they did not; for after love has joined them, they are apt to disappear from view. Even although he seems to tell you of their married state he is in reality telling you nothing. Anything that he learnt about matrimony he kept to himself.

He was a story-teller, and by that I mean he could (and, I think, still can) keep your interest alive and excited over the very tiniest events. He had in this a kinship with Anthony Trollope, whom he resembled in many things — in his stories too long drawn out, in his friendly but obvious moralizings, in his love for his own characters, and in a certain very charming and rather melancholy modesty — as though he would say, " I tell you these stories. It is kind of you to listen. I enjoy telling them to you. But life, in my own case, has not been quite as I represent it for these others. My own thoughts about my own life are nobody's business but mine." When Trollope wrote his *Autobiography* he composed as honest a book as there is in the English language, but he omitted from it everything that was deeply personal to himself. His spiritual, sexual, inner life is his own secret.

How different, naturally, from these our

present times, when boys of eighteen publish long works about their inner life and every novel is a more than sexual autobiography. Why should anyone complain of this? And, perhaps, only on this count — that the autobiography must spring from a most unusual personality to sustain the interest of a novel, and how many novelists have remarkable personalities?

It is of Marion Crawford's Roman novels that I am speaking. In them I found, in my lonely and self-frustrated boyhood, precisely what I needed. I was not myself handsome, courageous, successful. I was not in this at least self-deceived, but, because I had no friends in my own world, I sought them passionately elsewhere. Saracinesca, Sant' Ilario, those were the men for me! And Marion Crawford himself (I had cut out his photograph from one of Macmillan's catalogues) with his handsome, kindly countenance, his athletic habits (he could sail a little boat from one corner of the Mediterranean to the other, they said), his beautiful palace at Sorrento — he was the man for me too!

When a new novel of his was announced in the papers I prepared myself, as his humble servant, to do battle for him before the world. If in the *Academy* or the *Athenaeum* or the *Spectator* there were reviews of a mocking or contemptuous kind (as, alas, there sometimes were) I composed letters of rebuke and astonishment which, indeed, I did not post but conceived, mystically, must be known to the author and gratefully cherished by him.

I think he did what, oddly enough, only one other novelist writing in the English language has succeeded in doing (Henry James): he made Rome alive. Save for Stendhal's *Rome*, Crawford's *Ave Roma Immortalis* is, even yet, my favourite descriptive work on Rome — simple, sometimes melodramatic, but alive!

IV

I THINK that Ouida, and Ouida only, has ever considered Marion Crawford as a stylist, and she, in her study of him, in her *Critical Studies*, adopts that attitude of elder-sisterly admonishment, her favourite one to everything alive save only dogs.

Crawford, because he produced with military punctuality a new novel every autumn, was never taken with seriousness by the critics. He was a ' professional ' novelist — that is, he was a real and true novelist in the tradition of Richardson, Thackeray, Dickens, Balzac and Zola. And of course for the specialists he had no style — for he wrote as a plain man for plain men. Yet he wrote with exact and clear accuracy of the things that he described. Whether it were the sailing of boats in *The Children of the King*, New York Society in *Katharine Lauderdale*, Roman politics in *Saracinesca*, nunneries in *Casa Braccio*, he was always exact, clear and free of all nonsense.

This matter of style in the novel has always seemed to me wrongly considered by English post-War critics. A novelist must tell his story as clearly as he can and reveal his characters as living human beings. I have myself been told again and again that my own style is careless and that I don't know the meaning of words. Careless I may be, but I am often a good story-teller and after thirty years of it I know my business. In any case I try to describe things as I see them, as they really are to me. How I detest pose in a novel!

Good honest Marion Crawford, how excellent are your flat, unexciting, but truthful sentences beside the shams and gesticulations of posturing writing! Time deals with the shams, however. The poems, for example, of Stéphane Mallarmé, once considered remarkable because they were obscure, now that they are no longer obscure, are discovered to be empty and mediocre. On the reverse the stories and essays of Oscar Wilde, held, during the last thirty years, by serious critics to be the superficial poses of a man who was remembered only because of his tragedy, are now discovered to be filled with true wisdom and to include a deep and revealing philosophy!

So it may be that one day Marion Crawford, because he was an honest writer and could tell a story and knew about all kinds of things from sailing a boat to the lonely terrors of a murderer, will return. He was a minor novelist, he had talent, not genius — but what a debt we owe to the minor novelists! Yes, even of England alone, saying nothing about the Daudets and the Sologubs and the Howells and the Nexös of other countries. To Mary Shelley, G. P. R. James, Miss Ferrier, Miss Eden, Henry Kingsley, Harriet Martineau, Mortimer Collins, Rhoda Broughton, Mary Braddon, Charlotte Mary Yonge, Laurence Oliphant, Mrs. Oliphant, Olive Schreiner, C. E. Raymond, Israel Zangwill, Maurice Hewlett, Mrs. Humphry Ward, Arthur Morrison, Lucas Malet, Gilbert Cannan, Zack, John Oliver Hobbes . . . I take off my crumpled black hat and make my brotherly bow!

And here was the sallow Roman lady in the dark little shop, sprung straight, I must imagine, from Francis Marion Crawford's fecundating loins! Not that she knew it — knew in fact the alarming truth that she was, for one human being at any rate, a character from a novel not yet written and never to be written! I could imagine meeting her wispy and brow-beaten little husband, with his anxious eyes and placating mouth, putting my hand on his shoulder and saying to him, " Eugenio, my friend, rise above your fears, for this lady, your wife, is not real at all. Do not quiver when she turns her eyes upon you or pretend, in your mutual bed, to be sleeping when you are not, for your Benedetta is not real. She is *only* in a book. And even that is not so terrifying, for the book as yet has not been written."

I could see her, as I asked for the drawings, listening darkly in another *Taquisara* or *Pietro Ghisleri*, listening for the cries of her victim who shortly will be poisoned by the vegetable soup even now smoking on the dining-room table. . . .

But all she said to me as she showed me the drawings, in an English remarkably free from accent was: "Three lire. I have a case full of drawings here if you care to see them."

" You speak English remarkably well," I ventured.

" I ought to," she said. " I was born in Surbiton. I married an Italian. I've been here twenty years."

She smiled and yawned. She was full of motherly charm.

I carried under my arm the first yellow-covered volume of Zola's *Rome*, which I was reading exceedingly slowly because my French was but halting. The Abbé Froment had for three days now been staring at Rome from the top of the Janiculum.

" You read French? " she said, as the mother of some nice little boy might say to another little boy.

" A little," I answered modestly.

" Well, I don't know when I'll see Surbiton again. It's changed a bit, I shouldn't wonder. Ever hear Marie Lloyd at the halls? "

I wasn't sure but that that queen of subtle innuendo might not be dead, but I hated to distress this exile from home, so I lied brazenly.

" I saw her just before I left England."

" You did! Ah, she was the one. No one like her in Italy." She became strictly businesslike. " What about seeing the other drawings? There's dozens of them."

But I thought it wiser not. I knew my own weakness. Already on a number of occasions, although possessing no income to speak of, I had found myself with hot cheeks and a thumping heart, suddenly in the street, having spent in a

shop exactly twice as much as I properly possessed.
I knew well, even then, that delirious longing,
that crazy forgetfulness of everything save the
desire to possess, that lust of acquisition. . . .

So I said — no, that was all that I would be
wanting. I held the copy of Raphael's drawings
in my hand before it was rolled up and confined
within the brightest purple tissue-paper and tied
with pink string.

Enchanting page of mothers and babies! Babies
running and babies falling, babies laughing and
babies crying. Four mothers and three possible
fathers, although one of the fathers was no more
than a magnificent torso, stretching across the left
side of the back of the sheet. And one Madonna
of exquisite beauty in the right-hand corner, a
wreath of flowers set a little crookedly on her
head, a child, the merest child, but holding her
baby with watchful care, and the baby tottering
on its tiny feet, leaning forward, waving — waving
to its father perhaps, whose tremendous chest and
arms were fixed for ever on the top of the page.

Only one baby was crying and he had one eye
inquisitively turned to something or someone
who, new on the horizon, might be the very thing
that he wanted. The theme was the child's delight
and the mother's care, and I could, without too

much fancy, see Raphael himself stopping at the street corner and smiling as he watched the child in its joyful struggle to escape its mother's arms.

All this for three lira! I paid my money, I took my purple roll, I said that I hoped my hostess would soon see England again.

" Well, I don't know. I expect the country's changed a lot. I haven't been back for twenty years. I like the sun. We never had any sun in Surbiton, except in the summer, and then it was so hot you wanted to get to the sea. . . ."

V

IT happened therefore that I reached the little restaurant with my Zola and my drawings, and Mr. Montmorency shook his head at the first of these.

"Scabrous," he said. "That's what Zola is. Dirt. Couldn't keep his hand off dirt. What are you going to have now?"

I thought that I would have some fruit. A fine bowl of oranges, figs, pears and bananas was placed in front of me, and without a moment's delay Mr. Montmorency helped himself to the largest pear. He then made an extraordinary statement.

Dropping his voice a little he confided:

"I was once a clergyman. Church of England. I was a curate at Little Fieldway in Wiltshire."

Roman Fountain

You would have supposed that he was confessing to me something extremely disgraceful. His eyes searched mine anxiously. His unshaven chin seemed to flush beneath its grey shadow.

"Oh, I've stayed in Wiltshire two or three times," I said light-heartedly, to cover any shame that he might be feeling. And indeed I had. Some fragments — scent of mimosa, trees blowing in the wind, names from the Greek mythology, *The Chaplet of Pearls*, the long haunted passage where if you listened you could hear carriage-wheels and the postilion cracking his whip — these fragments from Longbridge Deveril where, as a small, grudging, rebellious, paying guest, I had spent my holidays with a kind clergyman and his family who were all so deeply learned that they called their dolls Achilles and Hector, Troilus, Pandarus and Cressida, and the clergyman's wife read us a chapter from *The Chaplet of Pearls* every Sunday and we had a chocolate each at the end of the chapter. Edward, Elsie, Dorothea — here now, after forty years, I greet you!

"Yes," I said. "I know Wiltshire quite well."

"Do you? But Little Fieldway. You wouldn't know it. Although it had a very fine church — Norman tower. I put the choirboys into surplices

and the villagers didn't like it. There was a
Colonel Thomas—— "

" Was that why——? " I asked, pausing
delicately.

" Well. That — and other things. I had
trouble with my Bishop . . . my enemies made
up stories. The singing was very good. I trained
the choir myself. They objected to my writing
poetry."

" Why, surely—— "

" It was a pity. I published two sonnets in a
magazine. Not under my own name. They *were*
a little free perhaps. Looking back now I can see
that they were a *little* free. . . . And then there
was a girl . . . oh, well — what matters it? I
was unfrocked if you want to know! Yes, I was.
A monstrous injustice! "

He glared at me. I saw to my astonishment
that his eyes were full of tears. He took another
pear and began to gulp it down, skin and all.

I was terribly sorry for him. I didn't mind
what he had done. I was very broad-minded, and
pleased that I was. I struggled to think of the
right thing to say. It wasn't easy.

" After all, if you weren't *meant* to be a clergyman, perhaps it was better. My father wanted me
to be a clergyman, but I saw that it wouldn't do."

He was already brightening. His eyes were dry, his mouth moist with pear.

" No. You're right. But I was an excellent preacher. People came from miles on a Sunday. I gave it them hot and strong, I can tell you."

The meal was over. I began to consider the bill. But Mr. Montmorency had still something to show me. He began to feel in his pockets, all stuffed with different articles.

It was with him that I encountered for the first time a phenomenon that I was frequently to witness again. There is a kind of human being who, like the snail, carries his house with him. His lodging is for ever impermanent, a back street, a bed-sitting room, here today, gone tomorrow, and so that he may be always in readiness, he carries about his person all that he may immediately need — old recommendations from friends now possibly with God, faded testimonials, a love letter, a dog-eared snapshot, a tattered notebook with addresses, a bill or two, and even, it may be, a collar in a piece of paper, a couple of handker-chiefs and a pocket razor.

Mr. Montmorency was of this tribe, and out of his pockets popped, for brief exciting moments, the oddest things — I can see now a toothbrush, a dog-collar and a small dry sponge, but perhaps my imaginative recollection betrays me.

It does not, however, betray me in the least concerning his ultimate production. He nudged me, drew a little closer to me, glanced around the restaurant, then, in the cup of his hand, displayed to me a series of indecent photographs, shabby, dog-eared and wearily ashamed of themselves.

"You can have the lot cheap," he said in a seedy whisper. "Dirt cheap — I'm tired of carrying them around."

At this point I should, I suppose, have got up and left him, revolted to my very soul. I should, at least, have behaved as Colonel Newcome did to the hoary, trembling old Captain Costigan. (I never liked Colonel Newcome from the very first moment of meeting.) But I did not. I examined the photographs with interest. Not, however, with much curiosity. Our admirable system of English public-school education had acquainted me, at the tender age of nine, with many things far worse than these.

"Oh no, thank you," I said politely, anxious not to hurt his feelings. "I don't think those things are very amusing. They're all the same, aren't they?"

"A bit monotonous," Mr. Montmorency agreed, putting them back into his pocket. He sighed.

His face now was wet and shiny, and the lock of hair that had been like dry seaweed half an hour ago had a dank, soaked look.

"It's damned hard to make a living," he said, eyeing my money with an eager stare. "I do what I can. But it's damned hard. That's what it is."

I paid the bill and he rose.

"Do you mind my coming a little bit of the way with you?"

I did mind very much and for one good sound reason: namely, that I was convinced that at the very moment when we started down the street he would ask me for money.

Now I couldn't afford to give him a penny and well I knew it, but my bones turned to water when anyone asked me for money face to face.

Is there anything more curious in human nature than this changing element of generosity and meanness? There are the rare souls who are wildly, even madly generous. For it is a sort of insanity. They are not happy unless they are giving somebody something, and they will give away things that are not theirs to give and will run into debt in order to give, afterwards avoiding the debt they actually owe.

And at the other end are the really mean, the misers, the clutchers and hoarders of investments and landed estate and possessions. Balzac knew all about these, but I must confess that, all through life and with a wide acquaintance with many different people, I have never known a real miser. Most of us are alike, generous one minute and mean the next. The two living persons for whom I care most are also the most generous persons I know, and that is in part, I suppose, why I love them.

It is not difficult to be generous to those you love. One of the exquisite pleasures in life is to see the look of happiness and joy in the eyes of a friend at the realization of a gift. And it is not hard to be generous when your heart is touched. You are pleased with yourself that you have so sensitive a heart and you are pleased with the suppliant for touching you. No, the difficult generosities are those that follow earlier generosities — the generosities from which all the colour is faded, the generosities that must be repeated because you are too weak in character to break the repetition, the generosities to those whom you suspect of becoming hangers-on but whom you have yourself *made* hangers-on, the generosities to those who are already deeply resenting you for being generous, the generosities to those who have changed, because you have been generous, from gratitude to patronage.

There is the further mystery of the Small Sum. To write a cheque is not so difficult if you have money in the bank ; to empty your pockets to pay constantly for someone who avoids the charge of taxis, theatre tickets, drinks and cigarettes, *this* is the irritating thing!

Much of this comes from a youth when every penny meant more than a penny. Arnold Bennett was a curious example of this. No man alive was more generous than he, and no one will ever know of all his secret charities, but I have seen him manœuvring with elaborate words and movements to avoid the paying of a taxi-cab.

Another friend of mine is very frank about the whole of this. His rule is very simple. He never gives *anything* away. He insists that to give away money is to ruin the recipient of it. But he is not a mean-spirited man. He follows a principle. He never gives money a thought except to see that he holds on to it.

One famous public man who is very wealthy and has given pleasure, by his taste and energy, to hundreds and thousands of people, told me once that he never supported the needy and the out-of-luck. " They will never come to anything or be the better for your help. I help those who are already getting on. Then you are doing something useful." A sensible rule, perhaps, but surely one very difficult to follow.

I believe that it is in childhood that the foundations of generosity or meanness are laid. I am absurdly greedy about certain foods, and all because I was starved at my first school. At this school (then a very bad one, now a very good one) there was a system known as ' Extras '. Richer parents paid more, and their fortunate sons were allowed ' Extras ' at breakfast. These ' Extras ' — one day a sausage, another a fish-cake, another a poached egg — were laid out in a row in front of the headmaster at the high table. When he said ' Extras ' the richer boys leapt to their feet, rushed to the dais and claimed their ' Extras ', while the poorer boys, who had only bread and dripping, watched them greedily. The smaller richer boys, however, seldom enjoyed their advantage, for as soon as they returned to their places the bigger poorer boys snatched their ' Extras ' from them. I was a smaller richer boy and, during the two years I was at this school, I never once, I think, enjoyed my ' Extra '.

That is nearly half a century ago, and still for

me sausages, fish-cakes and poached eggs have an unholy unnatural fascination.

In any case, to be mean is to be shut off from your fellow-men, to lose all true companionship, never really to be loved. To be wildly, casually generous is to be a fool. To be self-righteously pleased *because* you are generous is the worst fault of all.

I had, however, no intention of being generous to Mr. Montmorency. I began, in my secret heart, to beat up all my forces. I was resolved to be firm but kindly, and to give him the slip on the first opportunity.

He walked briskly along beside me.

" If you have nothing to do for a quarter of an hour I will show you what *I* think the most beautiful thing in Rome."

" Thank you very much."

" Oh, it's a pleasure. It's a Fountain — one that most people miss."

He had entirely recovered all his confidence. He was my patron, my guide of the moment.

" You know," he said very cheerfully, " this meeting has given me great pleasure. I have reached the age when I like the company of youth. They remind me of my own early days when all the world seemed in front of me."

Then he added, most unexpectedly:

" You don't think you're in any danger of becoming a bit of a prig, do you? "

This was so sudden and so surprising a blow that I stopped for a second in my walk, simultaneously resolving to show that I was not hurt, that I thought it a quite ordinary question, to which I would give a common-sense impersonal answer.

It was a blow the stronger because I had been so happily patronizing Mr. Montmorency, taking him under my wing as it were, and feeling greatly pleased about it. That *he* should ask me this question! Moreover, all my life long, I have been ready to believe at once almost anything anyone told me about myself. And why not? At that age, at least, when I considered myself, I seemed to have every possible quality and also the opposite of every possible quality. I was generous, I was mean, I was intelligent, I was stupid, I was educated, I was ignorant, I was loyal, I was a gossip, I was pure, I was obscene, I was active, I was lazy, I was sophisticated, I was immature, I was religious, I was pagan, I was affectionate, I was cold, I was adroit, I was clumsy, I was unusual, I was ordinary, I had no feeling about class difference, I was a snob, I was masculine, I was feminine, I was calm, I was hasty-tempered, I was ascetic, I was sensuous, I was a wit, I was a fool. . . .

The one thing of which I was quite sure was that I was an English gentleman, but that nowadays it was better not to be and certainly better never to think that you were!

But a prig? That was an awful thing! I could not say anything worse of anyone than that I thought him a prig. And yet I was not sure exactly what a prig might be.

"Oh, do you think so?" I said, with a gay indifference.

"I don't know, I'm only suggesting it. I've always been a great student of human nature. You're very young. You're almost the *youngest* young man I've ever met! So I hope you won't mind my remark."

"Oh, of course not. But what do you mean by a prig exactly?"

Mr. Montmorency considered, looking very wise indeed as he did so.

"I should say that a prig is someone who takes himself very seriously. Believes that he is better than other people."

This was awful. *Did* I believe that I was better than other people? I certainly believed that I was better than Mr. Montmorency.

" Oh, do you think so? I don't know what I believe about myself. I think I'm very ordinary."

This was a lie, and Mr. Montmorency, who now seemed as sharp as a needle, at once detected it.

" I don't suppose you do. Nobody does that. People couldn't live if they did."

" What makes you think I'm a prig? "

" You are very solemn about yourself, aren't you? You were shocked by my showing you those postcards, although you were determined to show that you weren't."

There I was certain that he was wrong.

" Oh no, I wasn't. Not in the least. Only I thought it a pity you should waste your time with such things."

Mr. Montmorency suddenly looked very dejected.

" You're right. You're perfectly right. I haven't any shame left. When I see a young man like you I think of what I might have been, and then I'm irritated. I've let myself go to pieces." He cheered up again. " It doesn't matter. I shall turn the corner. All I need is to find the right place for my abilities. I shall return to England at the first possible opportunity. All I want is a hundred pounds."

Roman Fountain

The moment had come then! I knew exactly what his next words would be.

" You couldn't lend me a hundred pounds? I'd pay you back in instalments."

" I'm afraid I couldn't," I said, feeling deeply ashamed of my firmness. " I've barely enough to get home with."

" Never mind," he said cheerfully, and I saw that he had made the same request of many persons before. " If, when you get home, you find you have it lying around — even fifty would do — send it along."

I realized then, what I have found since to be a universal law, that if you refuse a borrower he likes you all the better for refusing him, while if you give him the money he thinks you a fool.

This little matter happily concluded, I was able to attend to the beauty of the scene.

There are many ways of being a traveller, but the *great* division between one traveller and another is visiting foreign places with knowledge, and visiting with no knowledge at all. Both are good. *With* knowledge, you observe and note a thousand things that more ignorant you would miss. Every church, every monument, every picture is a mine of information. You dig and dig, and your clever excavations fill you with pride and self-satisfaction.

Roman Fountain

Without knowledge you move in a wonderful country, filled with surprising apparitions belonging not at all to your ordinary everyday world. Places are not places but sudden miracles having no relation at all to facts or dates or any kind of geography. On this first visit to Rome I knew nothing about Rome. I had my guide-book, but as soon as I looked at it I was lost in a multitude of confusing facts, and always the things that I didn't want to see were the things I saw.

I have always been stupid about maps, which never show me the places for which I am searching. My present geographical knowledge of Rome was based on some four or five places that seemed to me to be of infinite unrealizable distances the one from the other. My map of Rome was something like this:

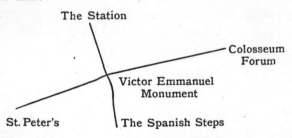

I walked, then, in a miraculous place with a miraculous name and I might see anything at any time anywhere.

Roman Fountain

And now I realized the light.

Roman light has, it seems to me, a different quality from light in any other place. The light in Africa is clear, without mercy, so powerful that you too feel powerful. The dim light of an English spring day is germinating light, rich with seed, promising flowers through rain. The light of Russia pouring down upon steel-silver snow is ancient and boundless. The light of Egypt, as you wake in early morning on the Nile, is fresher than any other in the world, and is like the *beginning* of the world. The light in California is seasonless and thin, but eternal. It seems there impossible that it should ever be dark.

The Roman light, except in July and August, when it is not to be borne (although at evening it is blessedly cool), is light *upon* light, veils of light, each veil clear but, in colour, transmuting substances of stone and mortar and marble to qualities of light. On a dark sombre day in Rome, the whole town changes and sinks into a kind of apathy, as though Rome said, " I will do nothing about this but wait until light returns again."

During the spring and the autumn Roman light has a life of its own, as though, in the sky, there was an activity quite independent of the earth.

Roman Fountain

When you are on one of the Roman hills you seem to be in a world of light that is neither the world of the earth nor the world of the heavens above, and, from the Janiculum, I have seen Rome soaked in a light that removes it both from earth and sky. Florence and Venice, the two other most beautiful towns in the world, are often unreal because of their beauty, but they live in *one* light which is a miracle but a reasonable miracle. The Roman light gives you three worlds, and the best of these is the one that you never see but know to be there.

I had been intent on my talk with Mr. Montmorency, and so now, when I forgot him and looked about me, I was surprised by a sudden glory.

How many times since then I have tried to recover the streets and houses between the little restaurant and the Fountain! But I can recover nothing. The beauty and amazement that I felt then I never quite caught in Rome again. It belonged partly to my youth, perhaps, my inexperience, my readiness to be exalted. But I remember that I wondered then, as I have often wondered since, at man's capacity to be astonished and transformed, at least for the moment, by sudden beauty.

It would be so easy, surely, for the world to

have been made quite other — to be a place of common grey with trees like telegraph poles, walls of dead metal, the hills of grey ash, the fields of flaccid moth-wing. There could be ugliness everywhere, no changing seasons, the yellow of a fog without its thickness.

Or, more probably, there might be this world of beauty and ourselves with no eyes to perceive it. Or, beyond that, we might perceive it and it might raise in us no sense of wonder, no desire to praise, no longing to make ourselves part of it, to contribute to it however humbly, no conviction, at sight of it, that this beauty is but the promise of some other and more lasting beauty.

There are, of course, some men and women in whom beauty raises no sense of wonder, like the young American in whose company I saw for the first time the incredible splendours of the Grand Canyon. Over the edge he peered and then said heartily, " Gee! Some ditch! " But that may have been simply his method of expressing his deep and spiritual feelings.

Had I a wish to be granted it would be that, allowed tolerable health, I might live for ever, if only the seasons still return and the sea is alive in all its manifestations and the hills stand firm in their glory.

Roman Fountain

I have been told that this wish is a selfish one. I should pray for the betterment of Man and the coming of the Kingdom of God upon earth. And so indeed I do. I have been told that I should, after two or three hundred years or so, weary of the spring and be discontented with the crocus and the summer rose. But as, with every increasing year of my life, I have loved these things the more, I think that in half a thousand years I should at last begin a little to understand them.

In any case, here, on this afternoon in Rome, I lifted up my eyes and greeted the light.

This day was towards the end of March and I fancy that it is during the last fortnight in March and the first fortnight in April that Rome is, of all the year, at its loveliest. Then there have been days of rain and the tramontana has blown and there have even perhaps been storms of hail. The light comes, after the rain, and sweeps the Roman world into a blaze of glory. The flower-beds on the Pincian exult and all the gardeners in the Borghese Gardens work like mad. The little lake there is alive with the chattering of ducks, and the children happily defy their nurses.

On such a day what Mr. Montmorency showed me was, I suppose, above its customary self. I saw the little Square as though it had been let down from heaven in a sheet. One long wall of building wore that colouring of red burnt by the sun into faded orange that is Rome's especial contrast to the silver-grey of her tarnished stone and undying marble. You may see it, before the sun has got to work on it, in the new red buildings of the Foro Mussolini, and very ugly they are, and you may see it, *after* the sun has burnt it, in the wall to the left of the Trevi Fountain, and there its orange-amber colours the waters of the fountain in the evening when the lamps are lit.

At the head of the Square was a little church with a faded yellow hanging in front of its door, a tower with a bell, and a kind of imitation of Michael Angelo's ' Moses ' (at any rate a saint with a beard) over the door.

The Square was cobbled and at the lower end of it were a stand massed with carnations, spring blossom and tulips, a number of small shops, an iron shop, a tobacconist's and a haberdasher's. In front of the haberdasher's there was a shoeblack.

In the middle of the Square was the Fountain.

The Fountain represented a Triton blowing his horn, and two children, each holding a fish. The figures, exquisitely carved, were of blue-grey bronze. The Triton, although his features were blurred by time, expressed magnificent joy and confidence. He seemed to be summoning with his horn all the company of gallant and triumphant men there were in the world. The carving of his back and loins was so vigorous that he appeared to be about to leap from the Fountain and stride from one end of the city to the other. The children also in their beautiful symmetry of limb and gesture expressed the climax of joy and energy. It was as though the three of them had at that moment heard news so excellent that they were transported out of themselves and could scarcely control their ecstasy. The waters of the Fountain leaped into the air as the waters of the Roman fountains so exultantly do.

It was the time between one and three when Rome takes its siesta, so that there was no one on the move, and even the cats, who in Rome are as inevitable as night and day, sat like little cat-statues carved into forms of light by the sun.

" I think," Mr. Montmorency said, " that this is the best Fountain in Rome. It is better than the Trevi, better than the ' Turtles ', better than any fountain anywhere. But no one ever comes to see it, no one ever writes about it. That is perhaps because it is not by Bernini. It is certainly *not* by Bernini."

Roman Fountain

" Who *is* it by? "

" I don't know. I have asked, but nobody seems to know. It is not in any guide-book. I have never seen a photograph of it."

" Why don't you photograph it? "

" I shouldn't care to. I might never see it again if I did."

Anyone less like a mystic than Mr. Montmorency in his shabby grey suit and dirty collar (although mystics *do* have dirty collars) you'll never see. But his voice had reverence and his mien was modest.

I wasn't, however, giving him a thought. I was thinking to myself, ' This is the best moment of my life. I shall never be so happy again.' I wanted to enclose this moment in a box and carry it away with me — all of it, the light, the colour, the Fountain, the church, the cats, the flowers — and **so** perhaps I did, for now, after all these many years, I can unpack it all and stare — stand and stare as though I had never moved away.

Perhaps that is so, and life since then has been a dream.

" I shall come back here tomorrow," I said.

" I don't expect you will. You have other things to see."

" Nothing as good as this."

" Then don't come back," he said. " The second time is always a failure."

As we walked away he said:

" If when you get back to England you find you have thirty pounds to spare, that would be better than nothing."

(He was like a friend of mine who, once, when I lent him fifty pounds, repaid the debt in the easiest fashion. After six months he wrote: ' I shall soon be sending you the forty pounds you lent me '. Then six months later he wrote: ' I haven't forgotten the thirty pounds '. Then, a year later: ' The twenty pounds you so kindly lent me I'll be sending very shortly '.)

Soon after we parted. I never saw Mr. Montmorency again.

VI

I PAID four visits to Rome between this first one and the present Papal adventure.

Three of them were of small account. One was of two days only and I remember nothing about it. Of the other two I can recollect a visit to Tivoli, a terrifying hour in the Catacombs, and a concert of Palestrina's music. During all of them I was surrounded with friends and busily occupied with a social life which in past days I mistakenly thought both important and amusing.

The fourth visit, however, was one of the luckiest and happiest things that ever happened to me. I brought my mother to Italy. Not very long after it she died, and it was a miracle of good fortune that we experienced this wonderful journey together just in time.

My mother was a little over seventy years of age and very frail and delicate. She had been to Italy before with friends, but never with me. We brought my car, which someone drove for us. We visited Pisa, Siena, Assisi, Rome, Florence and Venice.

It was to my shame that I had not taken her on many such expeditions before. The whole family had its summer holiday together, but this was always in the month of August and then it was too hot for Italy. Moreover my mother was an intensely proud person and hated to think that she should impose on anyone's freedom. Then, too, she must look after the house in Edinburgh, and I, occupied busily with my own affairs, would think that she was busy too.

It was, alas, not until the last few years that my mother and I came truly to know one another. In my youth I understood neither my father nor my mother, and they, on their side, found me difficult, conceited and uncommunicative. Until I was twenty-three or so they had wanted me to be a clergyman, and I did indeed try to become one, going, for a whole year, to the Mersey Mission to Seamen in Liverpool.

Roman Fountain

But nothing could kill my passionate determination to be a novelist, and they, with perfect reason and justice, could see nothing in my early outpourings that warranted this ambition. My father pointed out to me that there were a great many writers in the world, fighting and struggling, and that unless I was sure that I was to be another Robert Browning or another George Eliot, I would be wasting my time. I did not want to be another *anything*. I simply wanted to write novels. Yes, but I had no money, nor would anyone give me any. On what would I live? And so I surrendered, outwardly at least, and went to the Mission to Seamen.

For that life I was altogether unsuited. I did not want to make the seamen any other than they wished to be. I sympathized with them in their weaknesses and considered that most of them were better men than myself, which indeed they were. Moreover I wrote at every spare moment. Nothing discouraged me. I sent my first story to Ian Maclaren, who was very kind to me in Liverpool. I said: " Father wants me to be a clergyman. I want to be a novelist. Please read this and tell me what you think."

He did read it and answered me on a postcard: " Think you'd better be a clergyman."

Roman Fountain

It made no difference whatever. I *knew* I was going to be a novelist and was young enough to be certain that I would be a good one. No one else alive in the world thought so, however, and my father saw me wasting my time over nonsense.

My mother was, I think, more perceptive, although I did not realize that at the time. My father developed, during his life, from a rather narrow eager clergyman into a saint. He had the most beautiful character, utterly honest, pugnaciously courageous, a laughing, joking lover of life, pleased, like a child, by the smallest pleasures. He was so completely unselfish that I never knew him buy anything for himself or put himself first in anything. He had a wonderful zest in life and so simple and direct a belief in God that he never had any anxiety about anything — and this could at times be extremely irritating to his family. He had no idea about money at all and never carried more than a shilling or two in his pocket. When afterwards he became Bishop of Edinburgh he exasperated, I am sure, the Scottish financiers who had to do with St. Mary's Cathedral, by beaming on them and saying that God would provide. As a matter of fact it was he who, by his energy, raised the two towers of St. Mary's. No one else thought that it could be done. I have never known any other human being who deserved so truly the title of ' Man of God ', for he *was* a man, every inch of him. His sturdy thick-set body was a man's body with a man's impulses, but I cannot conceive that anyone ever dared to be filthy or obscene in his presence.

He was so utterly normal that he knew no half-shades, but he never turned from any sinner. Certain sins were so incomprehensible to him that he could not believe that the sinners had really committed them, even though done under his eyes.

He was devoted to his family and would defend them like a hearty, jolly, but actively attacking lion. After my novel *The Cathedral* appeared, Dean Inge criticized it in one of the papers. A few days later a very well-informed letter appeared answering the criticism, signed ' A Clergyman '. It was years later that I learned that it was my father who had written this letter. He himself never told me.

He had the shyness about his feelings and a dislike of anything exaggerated that belongs to the Walpoles, who are very English, very angular, very traditional. The Barham-Carlyon strain on my mother's side was much more romantic and emotional.

What my father in fact lacked altogether was any kind of aesthetic. Books, which he loved, music, painting, he judged only morally. Beauty was for him good conduct.

It seemed to me then, as it seems to me now, that the artist has nothing to do with good conduct. If he is a great artist, the world that he creates, whether in music or writing or painting, will be a great world and will therefore obey a tremendous moral law. What have the Beethoven Ninth or Michael Angelo's ' Dawn ' and ' Dusk ', or *Anna Karenina* or *King Lear*, to do with good conduct? They are finally on the side of the Angels, because the Angels are greater than the Devils, but not Beethoven nor Michael Angelo nor Tolstoi nor Shakespeare thought of anything but their creation. And the lesser artists must *try* to create great worlds even though they know that they cannot. Hope ever springs anew in any artist's breast.

My father deeply suspected the artist, as most normal healthy English people do. And it is right that they should. For the true artist is an amoral, egoistic, untrustworthy creature with whom no decent person should have anything really to do.

My father liked books that did good. I can see now my father and mother, on some summer holiday, sitting together under a hedge in a field, father reading *The Egoist* to mother. Father thought *The Egoist* one of the most moral books ever written, and so perhaps it is, and it is one of the things wrong with Meredith's novels that he will be for ever preaching at us.

My mother was different. She learnt, I think, very early in her married life, that there were some things in her nature that she must conceal. She loved my father devotedly, but she was an ironist and even, sometimes, a cynic. She knew that any kind of irony disturbed my father, even bewildered him. She found very few people throughout her life who understood her at all, and, as she was very proud, she became shy and reticent.

She had lived, the daughter of a doctor in Truro, a very retired life. She and my father were both very young when they were married in Truro Cathedral. My father was the first Precentor there. Then, almost immediately, he was appointed to a living in Auckland, New Zealand, and out there they journeyed. Half a century ago, that was no easy voyage. My mother had been told nothing about sex at all, and my father knew little more than she. When they arrived in New Zealand it was to meet a rough Colonial society — kindly, willing, but very different indeed from the gentle Victorian Cornish world in which my mother had lived.

There I and my sister were born. I think that in that first year of her married life my mother received a nervous shock from which neither her body nor her spirit ever quite recovered. My father loved her dearly but was, in those years, a young man, full of energy, but neither very subtle nor very perceptive. In any case he had a very difficult piece of work in New Zealand and he enjoyed his triumph over the difficulties.

My mother was always, from that day until her death, a rather lonely person, and she never led quite the life for which she was intended. She was, in spirit, an artist. She painted a little, she played the piano a little. She was an amateur always and she never had time to learn, but there was something about her painting, something about her piano-playing, slight though they were, that was original and her own. Like my father she loved little pleasures almost passionately, but, also like my father, she was an alien in the atmosphere of worldly affairs.

She was haunted, until her death, with the fear that there was not money enough, and after she was gone we found that there was more money than she had had any idea of. She was always a spirit from some other world, sojourning in this one, and, because she had great courage, making the best of this one. But she never truly belonged here. Every day of her life she must force herself to innumerable terrors that need not, truly, have been terrors at all — a clergyman coming to stay, a dinner-party, a journey, some sharp modern people to face, a tale of cruelty or an injustice or simply a servant to confront about some error or rudeness.

Whenever this apprehension left her, whenever she felt physically well, she became a radiant joyful person to whom every little happiness was a fresh wonder. Then her generosity of spirit was un-bounded, you could almost hear her clap her hands like a child. Beauty of scene, beauty of character, beauty of the arts when she was free of her shyness and able to embrace them with all her heart, were to her like Heaven opening. As with many shy, apprehensive people she could never understand why life should be at once so menacing and so rewarding.

Unluckily, from the moment that I went to Cambridge, I was away from home a great part of the year. I was, as I have said, at that time fiercely ambitious and I prosecuted my career as though I were out to win a bet. Then came the Great War when I was, for the most of it, in Russia.

It was after the War, during this wonderful Italian holiday, that we came, at last, after all these years, to know one another. She was so happy during this journey and so free from fear that her spirit flew, like a bird, into the open.

Real love between two people (I am not speaking of physical passion) is a great mystery, but it must, in any case, have as some of its qualities reciprocation, humour, honesty, patience, unselfishness and pleasure.

It was when we were sitting in the Palatine Gardens, looking down over Rome on the day after our arrival, that I discovered something.

" You have always thought everyone a little ridiculous, haven't you? " I asked her.

" I find myself ridiculous."

" Yes, but Father, the family, relations, people who come to stay — you've watched us all and wondered how we could be so absurd."

She was very frail. I can see her now, in a dress of light grey silk, sitting in the sun, drinking in the scent of the flowers, seeing Rome in the misty light rather like a great figured plate with towers as horsemen riding (she said to me later that it was as though horsemen were for ever charging silently through Rome — horsemen of half a dozen civilizations), loving the dark steel thrusting of the pines against the sky — she so very very slender, her hands on her lap so thin, her hair under her broad black hat so white.

She smiled shyly.

" That doesn't sound very nice that I should laugh at my friends," she said.

" It isn't laughing at them as individuals — only at something in all human beings. Leonardo, Michael Angelo — they were often ridiculous and the more lovable because of that."

" I'm afraid I don't love many people," she said with a sigh.

" Nobody does."

" Your father does, and that's because he always takes them just as they are. I so often wish that they were different. But never so often as I wish that I were different myself."

" What would you like to have been if you'd had your way? "

My mother laughed. " Oh, completely different. I would like to have been one of those grand, confident splendid women who are afraid of nobody, whom everyone is delighted to visit, and who turn, at the last, into lovely old ladies full of graciousness and anecdotes."

" I would have hated to have had a mother like that."

" Oh no, you wouldn't. You have all been irritated again and again by my nervousness and shyness and the mistakes I've made. Do you remember once when we had some Bishop or other to dinner and some time about the soup your father called out to him, ' I hope you like the claret,' and the Bishop, blushing up to the eyes, stammered, ' I'm afraid it's port '? You gave me, I remember, a simply furious look. It seemed a great joke to your father. I suffered for weeks after."

" What a horrid boy I was! "

" No. But you'd been away from us so much. That was the mistake, I think. Although you *were* at home all those years in Durham and, I'm afraid, seemed to us very stupid and lazy. We were often in despair about you."

" Yes! — I heard you talking one night in the next room to mine and saying: ' What ever are we going to do about Hugh? I'm afraid he hasn't even the brains to pass the examinations for being a clergyman.' "

My mother smiled. " Well, you see, it's turned out all right after all."

" No it hasn't! " I cried. " I'm incredibly stupid and ignorant. I learnt nothing at school at all. All those years and all that money. I might at least have learned *one* foreign language. That would have been something."

" You seemed to us to do nothing but read novels."

" I never learnt *how* to learn. I can see myself now in that beastly dining-room at Durham sitting at the table trying to parse Virgil or Ovid. And I was kept in one whole afternoon, I remember, over one Greek accent. Greek accents seemed to me mad crazy things. I couldn't see why they need exist. I was made to play cricket, which I loathed. And yet now the *Odyssey* in translation seems to me a perfect wonder and I would rather watch a good cricket-match than almost anything. *Why* didn't they make us see the beauty of things? "

" Why didn't *we*? " my mother said. " We could have done so much at home. But we were both so ignorant too, your father and I. Here I am, well over seventy, and I'm still almost completely ignorant. I've lived all my life and I've learnt nothing."

" You've learnt everything," I said. " You are a charming companion, you ——— "

" Oh, but I bore most people dreadfully. All my life I have. I've always just seen them getting more and more bored. Of course some people are so charming and so intelligent that you just

listen to them enchanted. Father Waggett, or
Mrs. Benson, or your friend Miss Mayne, or Arthur
Benson — but with *them* you don't have to do
anything. They only have to be themselves. But
when *I* have to contribute I have nothing to give,
nothing at all."

I thought of the many times that people had
told me of the enchantment they had felt with my
mother, of her charm and delicacy and shy humour.
I said so.

" Oh, do you think so ? " She was delighted.
" But why have you never told me before? Why
has no one ever told me? It would have been such
an encouragement."

Why indeed had I not told her many things?
There had been always this horrible reticence, this
shyness of showing one's feelings. Why had I not
paid her compliments and made her feel her unique
enchantment? Why was it only now, after all
these years, that the barriers had melted, yes, here
at last, on the Palatine, melted in the warm misty
afternoon sun?

" I think," I said, " it was a little your fault,
yours and Father's. When you came home from
America and we all lived together at Durham, I
was like a stranger and you were both too terribly
distressed at anything I did wrong. The thought

of that distress was terrible to me and it made me angry too."

"We didn't know anything about children. And you were the eldest. We loved you and wanted to understand you, but we couldn't. You shut yourself away and disliked everybody."

"Yes. I certainly disliked everybody."

"Well, how lucky it is," my mother said cheerfully, "that now you *like* everybody! Or most people."

She was so charming, smiling at the primrose-sparkling haze, listening to the ringing of bells (how strangely seldom bells ring in Rome!), lost in happiness. I was very happy too and intensely quiet in my spirit.

My mother looked at me.

"What would you have been if you hadn't been a novelist?" she asked.

"There isn't a thing I could have been. Not a clergyman, not a schoolmaster. A bookseller perhaps, if I'd had some money. Nothing. Nothing."

She looked over to St. Peter's.

"Once — you might have been a monk."

"A very bad one." I nodded my head. "Then —- in the sixteenth century I would have been, if I could, Vespasiano."

"And who was he?"

"I know about him because I thought once that I would make him the central figure of a novel. Vespasiano helped to form Frederick, Duke of Urbino's Library. He was born at Florence in 1421 and died in 1498, so he knew all the best years of the Renaissance. The Duke of Urbino's Library was wonderful. For more than fourteen years the Duke maintained thirty or forty copyists transcribing Greek and Latin manuscripts. His library contained works classical, ecclesiastical, Italian poets, humanists. Every volume was bound in crimson, with silver clasps! the leaves were of vellum and adorned with the finest miniatures. Printing was beginning to be the rage, but the Duke would have died of shame had he had a printed book on his shelves.

"Vespasiano helped to form three of the greatest collections of manuscripts in Italy, and yet he may also have handled some of the most beautiful books of the Aldine Press. He stood exactly at the meeting of the old world and the new, dying just thirty years before the Sack of Rome. He was a great biographer, and what is more, in one of the most immoral and cruel worlds this planet has ever known he lived a pure and noble life. There! Now you see why I would have been Vespasiano if I could!" I stopped my pious narration and my mother said:

"I like to hear about good men."

But I had for the moment concentrated on myself. I stared at Michael Angelo's dome, for I had a moment of self-realization. I realized that my own passion for creative beauty was stronger, stronger by far than any other passion in me. Neither wars nor the rumours of wars could affect it. I wrote *The Dark Forest* in the front trenches before Tarnopol under fire when I was waiting for wounded, describing the events at the exact moment they were occurring. I spent an afternoon in the 'Hermitage' looking at the Rembrandts on a day of the worst week in the March Revolution. The night in Petrograd when, sleeping in the Propaganda Office off the Nevski, alone, I was threatened by the Red soldiers with instant death if I didn't reveal a hidden policeman (who wasn't, of course, there), I lost all consciousness of the event because I was deep in Conrad's *Some Reminiscences*. I could forget anybody or anything — Hitler, income tax, rheumatism (almost) —if I were in the middle of the Bargello in Florence, the National Museum in Rome, the Museum at Naples. Yes, Vespasiano collecting his Greek texts, Aldo producing his beautiful books on the best paper known as yet to man, make

Hitler small indeed, and the rape of Prague a filthy momentary incident (although history will always record it). And here was I, suddenly, sitting with my mother on the Palatine, realizing one of the foundations of happiness.

But realizing, with that, my fundamental, abysmal ignorance. I loved all creative beauty, I lived by it; it was the fiery flame of my little life, mental, spiritual and physical, and — I knew nothing at all, no history, no language, no science, no philosophy, and certainly — oh, most, most certainly — no mathematics!

I took my mother's grey-gloved hand and pressed it, for she was in the same boat exactly. She too loved created beauty wherever she might find it, and she too was ignorant. The pair of us, there on the Palatine, were as perfectly uneducated, as simple a know-nothing couple as you would find the world over!

" Vespasiano! " I said. " What a comparison! And I can't translate the simplest line of Greek correctly! "

She understood. We had a moment of perfect, felicitous communion, bringing us close together, warm in one another's company, loving and knowing one another now and for all time.

" Perhaps," my mother said, " we know more

84

than we think. It gives me great pleasure sometimes to find that other people are ignorant too.
Mr. Lloyd George, for instance, at Versailles, I'm
told, when they were making their Treaty, had
never heard of some quite well-known place."

"Yes, and a contemporary of mine who has
always patronized me wrote a preface to someone's book and congratulated the author on dis-
covering a beautiful unknown lyric — 'There
is a Lady sweet and kind'. When I read that
preface I had a *very* happy moment."

It was time to go. We stood up for a last
gaze over Rome, now smoking like a sacrificial
pyre.

"There's one thing I *do* want you to see," I said.

"What is that?"

"It is a beautiful fountain. When I was here
years ago, as a very young man, someone showed
it to me. It's the loveliest thing in Rome."

"A fountain? All the fountains in Rome are
lovely."

"Yes, but this has something that none of the
others has got. I will show it to you tomorrow."

But I did not. On the next day we did something, and on the day after that we did something
else. And on the day after that we went away.

VII

I REACHED Rome on February 13th, 1939, at
4.30 P.M.

As I write this date I feel its strange and sinister
implication. I do not know when, if ever, this
account of my Roman adventure will be published,
and if it is published, it may appear in a world
ravaged and temporarily, at least, ruined by war.
Or it *may* appear in a world from which war is
at last disappearing, and only because men are
brought practically to the point of realizing both
its impersonal horror and its endless futility.

But this account is *not* about war. Whatever
may happen before I have finished writing, it will
not be about war. It is about something in the
spirit of man that moves *inwards* rather than *out-*

wards, that has something to do with a world wider
and deeper and longer than any man-made war
can touch. It is the story of a search for something
that is a key to that world, the only world of final
importance.

But I have no wish to be pretentious or mystical
— if, that is, mysticism means something vague,
impractical, illusory. Mysticism to myself means
the life of the spirit, which is as real as the life
of the body, conterminous with it, but a life not
terminated by the disappearance of the body. This
is a perfectly practical, realizable life for myself.
There is neither humbug nor vagueness about it.
I am aware of it whenever I choose to look or
listen, and I am a blind and deaf fool that I do not
look and listen more often.

All the same, this is in no way a mystical
account, unless you call searching for a fountain
in Rome mystical. I will be practical, actual,
realistic. What *underlies* realism is for me, in life
and in all art, the interesting thing, but you needn't
bother about that here unless you want to.

From Venice to Rome I was the only passenger
in the plane. When we flew over the mountains
we reached a great height and I was given oxygen
to breathe. After leaving the mountains we enjoyed that very ordinary experience which, how-

ever ordinary it may be, always makes flying worth while. We sailed through that upper world of shining light, of stainless blue, that is always joyfully serenely exulting above the cloud barrier. That world of light and silence realizes exactly my childhood's idea of Heaven. " There's a home for little children," we used to sing in the kindergarten at Truro, and exactly *that* is what I imagined then, the place whither I would be borne when I died, a guardian angel on either side of me. On and on we would fly until at last we would see in front of us the jasper walls and the pearly gates. . . .

So on and on in the peace and the silence, alone in the sky, we flew, and below us the world, with hills and valleys, castles and palaces of fleecy wool, slowly heaved and shifted and stirred.

I looked down. I glanced at my watch. Soon we would be arriving, would make that sinking plunge through the wool, and the windows of the plane would be smoked and fogged by thin wet mist. The shiny Heaven of little children would be unreal and unbelievable once more.

I would be coming down into the Country of the Enemy. Oh! not in the conventional sense. Not because Signor Gayda had been rude to us in his paper or because Mussolini orated or because one day we might be at war with Italy. Oh no! nothing against the Italian people, or the German either for that matter. Nothing new at all in fact.

I had passed in and out of the Country of the Enemy ever since I could consciously remember anything. In my childhood that country had been because I hadn't a regular home. At my private school I had lived for a whole two years in the Country of the Enemy, never leaving it for a single moment. During my youth that Country had been my self-conscious awkwardness. During my first years in London it had appeared when I realized that many people who seemed to wish me well did not in fact do so. During the War I had visited the Country whenever I was afraid and whenever I hated the Germans.

After the War, the Country had existed for me in the post-War Disillusion, the grimy and cynical fiction, the neurotic nervousness of which Coward's *Vortex* was the symbol. And for the last five years the Country of the Enemy has been the spirit of bullying aggressive force which I have seen grow-ing ever stronger and stronger. Not at all the German and Italian people; not even Hitler, Mussolini, Goering, Goebbels, Himmler, Streicher, and Ciano — although I did see a photograph of Nazi officials in conclave the other day that would surely strike terror into any simple heart!

But, in truth, no personal feeling against any single individual or any group — no, the territory begins, you pass the border, like Childe Roland you press forward over dead men's bones, when you breathe for the first time the sultry and stifling air that is driving Schuschnigg mad in Vienna, that has imprisoned Niemöller although he was found guiltless, that made old Jewish men and women kneel down and clean the streets before a jeering crowd, that raped Prague, that has filled the civilized world with starving, homeless refugees — *there* is the Country of the Enemy, and, on that first downward lurch of the aeroplane into the damp and clinging cloud, I am perhaps drawing near to it.

I reached the Rome aerodrome in pouring rain at 4.30 P.M. I stood there confused. I had hoped that Hillman or someone representing Hillman would be there to meet me.

Bill Hillman was the representative of the Hearst Press in Europe and my boss until this job should be over. I had never seen him. I knew nothing about him at all. I had no idea whether he was old or young, fat or thin, kind or unkind. This was really my first venture into journalism proper since my youth. I was fifty-five years of age and therefore it was hard to learn new tricks. I had in me at this moment, as all my life I had had, supreme self-confidence and deep misgivings. I felt that there was nothing I couldn't do and also that my whole life had been one long trick, taking people in.

There was nobody there; the rain poured down. Four dreary men gazed at me drearily over a fence. Someone told me to take the General Omnibus into the centre of the town. So I took it and shortly afterwards arrived in that large Square with the great fountain, the arcades and the Baths of Diocletian, the Square near the station, my old friend. I stepped out of the bus, transferred myself and my luggage into a taxi, told it to go to the Ambassadors Hotel.

There I enquired for my room, was told it was ready for me, was taken up in the lift and, after the unlocking and blind-pulling and cupboard-opening by the page-boy, saw that the room was small, would probably be noisy at night and had a bed that would be a sofa in the daytime. The room seemed, in fact, shabby and unsatisfactory.

I was to remain in it for five weeks and it would develop a very strange and unusual character before I left it — but I didn't know that then.

Roman Fountain

To the left was a bathroom and in the bathroom a huge shining friendly bath. Because of the bath I said that the room would do. I was left alone, and then, almost at once, the telephone rang. I thought it was Mr. Hillman. My heart beat. My hand shook a little. Suppose that he were one of those sharp, kindly-savage Americans who bark like dogs, sit in their shirt-sleeves, curse and swear, chew the damp stubs of cigars. You've seen them in many films, but they are quite real in actual life. I knew several in Hollywood and liked them. But not to work with. I simply didn't know where I was. I was lazy beside their activity, and active beside their laziness. It was all ' Dames ' and ' Dollars ' with them.

They were so very kind; there was nothing they wouldn't do for you. And generous! How mean are the English in comparison! But human beings to them were of one dimension only: the lid of a chocolate-box if you were a woman, the skin of a boxing-glove if you were a man. No deeper. A one-dimensional world. Men with kind gestures, a miniature vocabulary and no souls. Scarcely bodies, but very clean underwear.

Now if Mr. Hillman was one of these I was due for an unhappy, unsatisfactory month. My work would be bad and I should grow as home-sick as I was during my last year in Hollywood — a dreadful, searing experience.

But it wasn't Hillman. It was Alfred Noyes. He was downstairs with Mrs. Noyes. Would I come down and have some tea with them?

I went down. There they were sitting in the reception-room of the hotel — a dreadful room, as such hotel rooms always must be, for they are filled with the ghostly voices of departing hotel-guests wailing, " We tried to be real people here but were, after all our efforts, only numbers."

Alfred Noyes and I had been pleasant acquaintances for many years, but our meetings had been few. I had always admired him for his integrity, the courage with which, quietly smiling, he had pursued his way through the modernist world.

He was fatter than when I had seen him last. I was fatter too. I knew that we liked one another and trusted one another.

Trust was needed, for I learned at once that he had come on exactly the same business as myself. He was to write for the American afternoon papers, I for the American morning papers. We were to see exactly the same things and extract out of them what we could. We were, in fact, to be rivals, and I knew enough of the literary world to realize now that opportunities would arise for jealousy, for suggestions of favouritism, for jokes about one another that, misinterpreted, would grievously wound. He was a Roman Catholic and therefore very much better adapted for this particular business than I.

I was tired with my long two-days flight, already home-sick, wondering why I had come. Then I looked into Alfred's face and was reassured. We were going to be friends.

Bill Hillman came in and I was reassured again. Physically he was like Mr. Pickwick without the glasses. His voice was soft and agreeable. He looked at Noyes and myself and I think was comforted. We were, all three of us, stout of body and avoiders of quarrels. We would do our best to be pleasant.

I found that, at once, without a moment's delay, we must go and see Pius XI lying in state and, directly we had seen him, write about it.

I had for the last twenty years led an extremely comfortable life and, except for the Hollywood adventure, been absolutely my own master. I felt now, standing there, smiling politely at Hillman, my first non-journalistic instinct to tell him to go to hell. I had that fuzzy dry-paper headache that so often follows a long flight. I was tired and a little sick. My clothes were horrible upon me. I wanted to lie in that wide, shining, non-journalistic bath.

Surely it was fantastic that I should be dragged at once, without a moment's pause, to see the body of the dead Pope! And then to write about it immediately afterwards! I needed time in which to assemble my impressions, or, rather, to allow *them* to assemble themselves. I couldn't go directly from St. Peter's and . . .

I murmured something, still smiling. And then I examined Hillman's face — chubby, genial. You might call it a Masonic or Rotary Club face, until you looked at the eyes and the mouth. Relentless. Almost fanatic. From that first moment I realized that Hillman was not in the very least what superficially he appeared.

So we went.

Inside a taxi, waiting for us, was Michael. Michael was a young Albanian and, I believe, a relation of King Zog. He was of course most innocently unaware of his royal cousin's immediate future during all the time of my stay in Rome, but, when he spoke of him, I always felt that he might at any moment be disappearing over the frontier with his crown, his sisters and his stocks. One had that feeling about him always.

Michael was slim and dark. He smiled during the whole of my five weeks in Rome. He also wore on every occasion a grey overcoat that fell to his heels and masked his shoulders with a ridge of iron. He also always carried grey gloves.

He was, from the beginning to the end, kind, helpful, unselfish to a degree, of the utmost practical service, and yet, I will admit, he was never quite real to me. He was a doctor with full degrees and, if I had met him in any other circumstances, he would have been of most positive reality. When we do meet again he will, I am sure. But he was throughout on the fantastic side of this adventure which, as it developed, became more and more like a picture by Breughel.

If he was never quite real to me, however, that didn't mean that I didn't become very fond of him. His goodness of heart will make me tender towards any Albanian I may ever in the future meet. However Italian they may be in their superficial government, they will for me have always something of Michael in them, Michael with his long grey overcoat and inevitable grey gloves.

When we arrived at St. Peter's Square we left the taxi and attacked the gendarmes. These attacks on the gendarmes were, I may here remark, incessant throughout the adventure.

Roman Fountain

The policemen of Rome are today very small, peaky, insignificant men and they wear a uniform that does not, I feel, suit them at all — soup-plate black helmets precisely resembling the hats of our policewomen in London. They look, in fact, very feminine. When, later on, I asked my friend Rosso why they were small and insignificant, he said that it was because it was generally held that to be a policeman was almost the lowest thing you could be, and that the sturdy Italians of the North did not wish to be policemen and they were therefore recruited from the Italians of the South, who were, in physique, little men. These little men like policewomen played a large part in my five weeks in Rome. If they liked you they were most amenable; if they didn't like you they were ferocious. The thing therefore was to make them like you.

I had my first example now of that undying opéra-bouffe element in the Italian character that makes them so irresistibly charming. Crowds of people were passing in under the pillars to pay their reverence to the dead Pope. Exactly where we stood, however, there was a gendarme who repeated again and again that 'Nobody could enter'.

When we represented that thousands of people

were entering, he simply repeated his formula. Six pillars down there was no gendarme, and all we had to do was to stroll nonchalantly along, discussing the weather, then skip round a pillar and there we were! We decided, however, that this would be undignified. Therefore Michael, as he was to do on so many future occasions, disappeared. What he did when he disappeared I was never exactly to discover, but always, after ten minutes or so, he reappeared grinning, and the way was made easy for us.

I asked him once what were his tactics. " The thing ", he said, " is to be agreeable to absolutely everybody. You can do anything in Italy if you are agreeable, nothing at all if you are angry."

On this occasion, when he reappeared, we marched up the great steps, by the Swiss Guard, slipped through a side door, and were at once inside St. Peter's.

I had been inside St. Peter's on several occasions as a tourist. For the tourist, St. Peter's is inevitably disappointing. Michael Angelo's Dome seems the only fine thing about it. Had it been completed as Michael Angelo designed it, it would indeed be the wonder of the world. But the Dome is the only thing that is his, and the rest of the Basilica is a sad evidence of what malice and the little minds of men can effect when they are determined to frustrate genius.

The interior is dwarfed by Bernini's great pillars; there is a chill in the atmosphere and there are never enough people there to give the place life.

But now I was no tourist. St. Peter's was to be my home for five weeks, and never again shall I think of it as cold and lifeless.

We, all of us, at once joined the black procession; it moved slowly and thickly like trickling treacle. The crowd was composed entirely of what used once upon a time to be called ' the working classes ' — women often with babies in their arms, young men and boys and old men in black clothes and with rough grizzled cheeks.

Once again Michael showed us the way and, slipping round two pillars, we quite suddenly found ourselves directly opposite the Chapel where the Pope was lying and a little aside from the crowd of people.

There he was in his gold mitre and gorgeous robes, lying in a slanting position, huge lighted candles on either side of him, four Noble Guards motionless like statues in splendid uniform, the Chapel barred in front of them so that no one could touch him and most certainly no one could bend down and kiss his shoe as some journalists afterwards reported they had seen. His face had been waxed, but already corruption could be seen to be ravaging it. He looked very mild, gentle, unimportant, and very, very dead. There was, in fact, no one there at all.

As I turned from my impertinent stare at that waxen mask I saw two tiny children near me, for the moment forgotten by their mother, playing ' tig ' round one of the pillars. They must have become well accustomed to playing this game on public occasions, for they were very clever in their quietness and secrecy. They were absorbed in it, but at the same time had eyes on their parents and moved like ghosts, smiling but so very silent that you could not be sure they breathed. But how alive they were! So two puppies or kittens might have played, but their individualities were so strong! I had never seen them before, I would never see them again, but I knew at once that the little thing with black hair and sharp sparkling eyes was a ' boss ', would strike out for everything that she wanted, would create scenes and disturb lovers and fight for her rights, while the larger plump girl would be kindly, acquiescent, obliging, contented. And in addition to these type characteristics there would be certain spiritual elements,

growing or decaying, that would make them
utterly different from any human beings on this
planet, before or after them.   As different, as
unique, as Michael Angelo and Milton and Dickens
and Cézanne and my gardener Frank.

How alive they were! and Pope Pius XI
was dead.

This was a platitude, and yet it was not one
when I returned to look into the Chapel again.
Suppose one of the Noble Guards sneezed! Suppose
the candles blew out! Suppose the Pope rose from
his slanting slab and asked for a glass of water!
How would everyone behave if he did?   They
would all scream and run, but it would be a great
landmark in history, February 13th, 1939.   The
day of the Miracle, when Pope Pius XI rose from
the dead.   What would he have to tell us?   But
he wasn't there.   Nothing was there but the
corrupting, rotting body, a body like any other
body, mostly water, hurriedly to be put deep,
deep into three coffins and lowered beneath
ground.   I thought of the wicked Alexander VI
who, after his death, had begun to corrupt so
quickly and so horribly that he could not lie in
state at all, but there under the benign, glorious
beauty of Michael Angelo's ' Pietà ' had been hurriedly crammed together (because the coffin was

found to be too short) and shoved, 'a liquid mass of putrefaction', into his box and scuttled away.

Had Pius XI been anything but this ridiculous chemical assembling of gas and water? Most assuredly he had — a good, wise, patient, kindly father of his people, believing devoutly in his own spiritual life and, in spite of his mountain-climbing and pleasure in his physical life, ready to fling it off at any moment like an old cloak.

One or two had loved him dearly as a person — I was to meet one of these in a little time: millions had loved him as a symbol whose human activities they also shared. But he was not here, not here as truly as his golden mitre was here, and, beside him, the motionless Noble Guards were wondering about the next meal, and whether it would be fine weather for the motor drive, and about the sciatic nerve in the left leg, and the overdraft at the bank.

The simple faces stared eagerly through the golden bars. This was the Pope then! They had seen him perhaps at a service or ceremony. They had thought of him as the Voice of God. They had tried to do what he had told them to do. It had been a comfort in their lives to be in contact through him with something that did not change, that did not fail, that did not appear in Tuesday's morning paper to be something altogether different from the thing that it had been in Monday's — something that promised them compensation one day for the roughnesses, the wearisome monotonies, the ingratitudes of this daily life. What they wanted was kindliness and reassurance. Pius XI had given them these things.

But he was not here. Where was the heart of the mystery? Why was I so certain of my own individuality, or rather so certain of the longing in me to reach my true and proper centre, to find my Fountain, to achieve reality?

Such stale, stupid words! Such platitudes! A longing for safety and reassurance that was created partly by fear, partly by sentimentality! Or was it? At least I might say that this search which ceaselessly demanded my preoccupation was for me a real search. And I could go by no other experience but my own. It was of no use for me to say that someone I knew had found the Fountain — it wouldn't be *my* Fountain that he had found. Or for someone to say that of course there *was* no Fountain.

No, for him mere foolishness. But I was myself, alone on this journey, and, again like Childe Roland, I must go on through whatever dark country because it was *my* journey and no one else's. The dead Pope told me only that Death is not there when the body dies, for Death is a power, a reality, a positive force, while here, in that decayed dressed-up corpse, there was nothing.

" The answer doesn't lie here," I said to Michael, and he, grinning, understanding nothing of what was in my mind, answered:

" I'm that damned hungry——"

We went to the Hearst offices and I shouted out my impressions while Hillman banged them down on to the typewriter.

That was difficult for me. I had no time to pick my words and into the middle of every winding sentence came the mosquito *ping* of the typewriter.

But Hillman was very kind. He only said that I must start every article with a bang. " In America, you see, they have so much to do and they'll buy five or six newspapers at a time and if the opening sentence of an article isn't arresting they won't go on with it."

" That's just too bad," I murmured, feeling that I didn't care a little tinker's curse whether they went on with the article or not. But that was wrong of me. I was there to do a job for which

I was being paid. So I must care for my job, honourably care for it.

From now onwards all my articles began: "I have today seen the most remarkable . . ." "Only an hour ago, seated in one of the Cardinals' thrones in the Sistine Chapel . . ." "Probably in no Papal Election until now has there been so astonishing . . ."

But, all the time, behind the echoing words and the hiccuping typewriter, was this vision of the corrupting purple stealing into the waxen cheeks.

Why did I feel as though I had been cheated? I had gone to see the Pope Pius XI lying in state. I had seen nothing but two children playing ' tig ' around one of St. Peter's pillars.

Back in my attic at the Ambassadors, I un-packed my things. Tomorrow very early I must be up and put on full evening dress for the Funeral. A humiliating, depressing thought. There were no flowers in the room, which, as yet, had neither soul nor character.

So I opened my small Russian fifteenth-century box and laid out my Lares. Ever since I could move about at all I had carried with me some sort of box containing my personal gods. Originally they had been sea-shells, a paper which I then thought (being ten years of age) asserted my right to an earldom, and a fragment of cedar-wood.

Now, for a long time past, my Lares had been a Netsuke of two Japanese wrestlers, a small porcelain bird with a yellow head and blue beak, a dark-green jade elephant and two small elephants of coral and jade, and a tiny landscape by Renoir. During my long American lecture-tours in many of the barest and most hideous hotel bed-rooms that the world contains, these Lares had asserted themselves against the telephone, the ash-tray, the loathsome black blotting-case and the Gideon Bible. Very successfully they had asserted themselves and most gratefully had I grown to love them.

I held the superstition (a grossly sentimental one) that they, in their turn, loved me. One does at least acquire towards the things that one loves a protective, cherishing, defensive activity.

Only a few weeks before my leaving for Rome I had discovered this very sharply. I had invited my old friend, Eddie Marsh, to lunch in my flat. In my own private heart I longed that he should see and admire my pictures. Since his last visit I had acquired some beauties — a Bellini, a Quentin Matsys, a Cézanne water-colour, a Renoir seascape.

Roman Fountain

On that morning before the luncheon I went around my room seeing that my pictures were in the best possible positions and addressing them. "You know," I said to the Bellini and the Renoir, "that of the people that come into this flat, many care nothing for you at all. Some care, but are anxious to show their own cleverness. Some don't care, but pleasantly pretend to. Today someone is coming who loves pictures, is wise about them, gets delight from them. This will be a great pleasure for you, so look your best and enjoy your treat."

Others were coming to lunch, but, as far as the pictures were concerned, Eddie was my only guest. All morning I was in a state of restless excitement: I resolved that I myself would say nothing about the pictures, would behave as though they did not exist, would wait for his own spontaneous expression of delight.

Eddie came, stayed two hours, and never once mentioned a picture or looked at one. He was not aware, I think, that there were any pictures there at all.

When he had gone I was in a furious rage. I went around apologizing to the pictures. "Don't be upset. I know it has been extremely disappointing for you, especially after all that I said.

But obviously Eddie knows nothing about pictures, or, at any rate, cares nothing. If he cares at all it is only for the miserable pictures that he has bought — and his chief pride in *them* is that he has never paid more than twenty pounds for any one of them. So don't, please, be disappointed. I'll think of someone to have here very soon who will make up for your disappointment." And indeed Albert Rutherston, only a few days afterwards, made up very handsomely indeed.

Poor Eddie! And he had in all probability left my luncheon party feeling that he had been the life and soul of it!

How often, I wondered, going a little farther, had I left a party feeling exactly the same thing, and how often, against all my knowledge, I had been counted a bore, a conceited ass, a self-satisfied sentimentalist! I should in fact have learnt a lesson from the very first week-end party I ever attended, up in Cumberland, and I aged about seventeen. I had been, I thought, on the Saturday evening, everything delightful; but on the Sunday morning, locked in the lavatory, heard my hostess and another lady discussing me while they arranged the flowers. And *what* they said! How often of course I have been a member of these post-mortems that dissect an absent friend, and

sometimes I have suddenly woken to the extraordinary unselfconsciousness of the company that
they themselves will very shortly be thus dissected.

We are all of us so relentlessly in the same
boat that we may as well be merciful to one
another — and we are, I think, more tolerant than
we used to be.

So are we all, no doubt, with our three selves:
the Self that acquaintances know, the Self that we
think we are, the Self that the very few who love
us know. I fancy that this third self is nearer the
truth than the others. Often a loving knowledge
is not very flattering, but the silly weaknesses, the
bad vices, the irritating tricks and mannerisms,
are considered with kindly tolerance, are even
watched over and protected lest they should pro-
voke others more brutal and more indifferent.

Before I went to bed the room looked Wal-
polian. On the table near the window were the
Renoir landscape, the china bird, the two Japanese
wrestling, the three elephants, the Russian box.
On the writing-table between the doors were the
few books that I had time to snatch for my journey
— *The Renaissance in Italy*, *Michelangelo*, both
Symonds; *Rome*, Zola; *Notre Dame*, Victor Hugo;
Dante — *Inferno*, Binyon; *Cities of the Plain*,

Proust; *Don Quixote*; Pepys' *Diary*; a volume of
English verse published by Gollancz; a volume of
Spinoza; Virginia Woolf's *Common Reader*; Eliza-
beth Bowen's *House in Paris*; and *The Forty-five
Guardsmen* by Dumas.

I don't know what kind of a collection you
would call that. I had neither the Keats nor the
Wordsworth I had intended to bring. I had
plucked the Proust, the Quixote, the Pepys from
the little shelf near my bed and then rushed down,
through the dark, wet, scented garden, to the
library and found the others haphazard. The
Virginia Woolf and Bowen were Penguins bought
at the Munich Air Station.

Very good they looked, all arranged between
the brown-and-white collapsible book-ends that
always travel with me. Especially was I glad to
see *The Renaissance*, which I had not read since
Cambridge days and had always intended to read
again. Symonds was, I suspected, a very much
better writer than present superior taste considered him. I hold him to be a brave, fastidious,
sensitive man. To publish the *Greek Ethics* book
in those Victorian days was as courageous a deed
as you could find anywhere!

And how friendly your own books are in a
foreign hotel! They are, you understand, as lonely

and uncomfortable as yourself, and you are of more value to them here than in the library at home where they are accustomed to be, and are sure of good treatment. It isn't merely fancy to suppose that they have their moods as surely as we ourselves have, that they can sulk and retire within themselves and stick their pages obstinately together and slip back into a shelf so far that you abandon the attempt to snatch them and choose another book instead. Some books are very much more sensitive than others. I have the *Don Quixote* that belonged to Charles Lamb, and a book that more heartily loves to be used I have never possessed. When you hold it in your hand you can swear that the polished brown leather of the cover takes on an extra glow, the rough page — it is a seventeenth-century copy — accosts your fingers with a friendly touch.

Half undressed, I leaned out of my window over the empty shining street, sorry for myself with home-sickness. I seemed to scent the flowers through the rain and touch the marble with cold damp fingers and push with my hand the slow, heavy leathern doors of the Roman churches — and I longed, I longed to be back at Brackenburn and watch the wild kitten dash across the lawn, and see the Lake, cup-shaped, waver with its silver

trembling lines under the wind, and stand on the
ladder in the library, reaching up for the thick
dumpy volumes of *Clarissa*, and hear the sheep go
complaining down the road, and crush in my
fingers the wet brittle leaves of Manesty trees.
. . . Oh, but I was home-sick, and the Roman
street blurred under my misted gaze and I pulled
my shirt over my head and cursed softly, and knew
that, for some reason, I was afraid — afraid of
Italy, afraid of Rome, afraid of not being with
my own people.

I was not afraid at six o'clock next morning
when I put on my evening clothes — I had only
that dusty, untidy sense of disorder that comes
with putting on evening clothes in broad daylight.

Down in the hall Hillman and Michael and
Noyes were waiting. We drove off to St. Peter's
and there, in the Square, met a kindly Monsignor
who was to lead us safely to our appointed places.
He had a gay, merry and slightly cynical air as who
would say: 'Men come and men go. Life is
pleasant for a moment, but not from any point of
view important. Ceremonies like these are a
trifle absurd.'

I was prepared to find this ceremony so. I
had now hanging over me the intolerable bore of

knowing that, in a few hours' time, I should have
to shout some comments on to Hillman's typewriter that would be ' arresting ' to the people
of America.

I felt soiled and drab in my evening clothes.
Moreover I had decided for myself last night that
the late Pope was no longer here; I should see
his corrupting corpse borne with much ostenta-
tion to its last station. I was already in the dilemma
of having, for pay, to be emotional about an emptiness — about nothing.

And then, as the smiling Monsignor led us to
our places between the Bernini pillars and the far
Altar, I was caught in a new atmosphere.

St. Peter's was alive as I had never seen it before.
The colour was superb: the deep dark-purple
hangings, the many candles in front of the Bernini
Baldacchino, the high gold catafalque, these were
a deep, deep background to the colours of the
motley figures that moved in front of it. Deep I
emphasize, for that was what St. Peter's for the
first time was. Chesterton it was, I think, who
said somewhere that it is as though a high wind
blows through St. Peter's because of the way in
which the garments of the statues are all swept in
the same direction.

This wind comes to a pause at the great baroque

Baldacchino of Bernini, designed by him for
Urban VIII. Here the wind ceases, for the myriad
candle-flames are still and, above, Michael Angelo's
Dome rises to incredible heights. I looked now
into that Dome, and at once we, all of us on the
vast floor, were pigmies — pigmies with immortal
souls? Well, it was a man who had designed that
Dome, an ill-tempered, grumbling, dirty-housed
old man who, were he moving now amongst this
same crowd, would seem the merest pigmy like
the rest of us.

I flew down from the Dome's centre to take part
in a twisted fantastic masque.

On every side of me were figures out of a dream.
Ladies in black mantillas and veiled, monks
wearing sandals, priests of every order, ebony-
coloured faces of priests from the Pope's own
especial Abyssinian college, clerical robes of
crimson, mulberry, purple-brown, grey, and laity
straight from Velasquez' pictures, and the Swiss
Guard, the Noble Guard with their crimson and
gold, gentlemen in stiff white ruffs and black knee-
breeches, soldiers holding high their glittering
pikes, and even a dwarf with red satin breeches.
Up and down fussy little gentlemen in modern
evening dress with military orders went, marshal-
ling discipline, but we were a world without

order.   We talked quite loudly, walked where
we pleased, pushed and scrambled and chatted to
strangers.

There was no sign in any face of sorrow or
solemnity.   The occasion was gay, unstudied, as
free as it was easy.   Only I noticed that through
the vast Basilica a different spirit ran.   The Basilica
was alive and was timeless.   I caught into my
imagination again that picture I had had on the
previous evening of the black corrupted body of
Alexander VI shoved furiously, stamped dis-
gustedly down, into the too-short coffin under the
lovely eternal resignation of Michael Angelo's
' Pietà '.

That ' Pietà ' was there now, only the length
of the Basilica away — there, with Michael Angelo's spirit proudly, fiercely guarding it.   For
he wrote his name on it.

Vasari recorded that

Such were Michelagnolo's love and zeal together
in this work that he left his name — a thing that he
never did again in any other work — written across
a girdle that encircles the bosom of Our Lady.   And
the reason was that one day Michelagnolo, entering
the place where it was set up, found there a great
number of strangers from Lombardy, who were
praising it highly, and one of them asked one of the

others who had done it, and he answered, " Our Gobbo, from Milan." Michelagnolo stood silent, but thought it strange his labours should be attributed to another: and one night he shut himself in there, and having brought a little light and his chisels, carved his name upon it.

' Our Gobbo, from Milan ' — how well I know him! I suppose that Michael Angelo cared no more than another man about his posthumous fame — that is he cared a great deal. So curious, so pathetic a desire that we should so earnestly long to be remembered after our death — only a little word, a passing thought — someone picking up an old book somewhere, glancing contemptuously in a gallery at the name beneath the picture! I looked up into the great heart of the Dome again and almost thought that I saw him there, frowning down upon us, scratching his untidy beard, wrinkling his shaggy eyebrows and grumbling, " As soon as I was dead they spoilt my whole design."

" I beg your pardon," said an American voice in my ear, " but you are standing on my toes."

There were many young priests from the American College and they were like schoolboys, finding absurd things everywhere but ardently devout also. I was wedged now in a crowd almost exactly opposite the Baldacchino, where the actual

burial would be, but round the corner away from
the Altar where the enclosure in the three coffins
would be. It was here and now that I noticed for
the first time the child-like irresponsibility and
sarcasm of the Italians — was surprised to find in
fact, in these superficial but significant moments
of observation, no difference at all between the
Italian of 1910 and the Italian of 1939.

I must break off here for a moment to remark
that my observation of the Italian during these five
weeks was indeed superficial, for I was hemmed
in and circumscribed both by the nature of my
job and by the very amateurish fragment of the
Italian language that I possessed. But the quest
upon which already I was engaged was soon to
declare itself three-headed. No foreigner at that
time in the spring of 1939 could enter Italy without at once asking this question: " Has Mussolini
altered the Italian character? Has he transformed
his people into stubborn, determined, heroic
fighters? " Abyssinia had been no answer to that
question. Spain had been no answer. *Upon* that
answer seemed, at that moment in the fantastic
historic panorama that had now been developing
for so long, the very peace of the world to hang.

Do the characteristics of peoples change? Of
the old stern, cruel, heroic Roman stock nothing,

I was told, remained in modern Italian blood. But
would I now discover that Mussolini had, in some
necromantic fashion, reintroduced it, bringing the
spirit of the old Roman time to stiffen this softness
of apprehension and idle pleasant kindliness? Was
Mussolini himself the old Roman? Certainly
Ciano, Gayda and the others around him were not.
Balbo perhaps? Ah yes, Balbo possibly.

Meanwhile, at this moment, it was as the cooing
of doves and the chattering of monkeys around me.
Everyone was very happy. This happiness came
partly, I think, from the fact that the crowd inside
the Basilica was, in a sense, an exclusive one.
Some four thousand people perhaps. Really
selective. Partly from the fact that nearly everyone was dressed up, a thing that the human being
loves. The monks and priests, of whom there
were thousands, were *not* dressed up, but they
had the pleasure of knowing that, for the moment
at least, they were in power. It was *their* show.
And they developed all around them that per-
vading spiritual reality — a reality so often notice-
able, recognizable in the Roman Catholic religion
when all the conditions should be so exactly
against it. I was to ask myself on many later
occasions what it was that they really believed
and how far I shared my belief with them (what

an impertinence, Ronald Knox would say, that I should presume such an attempt!), but today I was aware only of their kindliness, their benevolence, their child-like eagerness to see *everything*, to miss nothing at all, their quick eager smile if your eye caught theirs! It was as though they knew they had asked you to a party and did hope that you were having a good time!

I climbed some little steps and was wedged between a short stout official and a tall stout monk, wedged as though I were part of their bones and flesh, and they part of mine — while a lady in a black mantilla leaned a little forward from her seat just above me and, gently, unobtrusively, stroked the back of my neck with her hand.

Staring from here down the length of the Basilica, I felt that the great place had now come truly into its own. Surely the air had grown darker and thicker since my entrance of an hour and a half ago! The candles, like orange-flowers in a dusky garden, glittering before the Baldacchino, seemed to have increased their power. The great purple hangings were now closer together and more emphatic. You could hear the heart of the Basilica beating, and the crowd upon its floor seemed ever so slightly to rise and fall. That crowd was now of the Middle Ages — the crowd of Velasquez and Leonardo, Machiavelli and Cellini, Rembrandt and Greco. In the far distance you could see only heads forming a field as it were of dark broken peat. Nearer the Baldacchino the colour of rose and white, purple and gold, the gleam of the pikes, the glitter of swords, all cast as it were in disorder upon that marble floor, had a life, by accident, that was more real by far than any disciplined stage producer could ever create.

The faces were as the faces then had been — stupid, arrogant, kindly, resignedly old, cruel, greedy, noble, indifferently lazy.

The monk at my side laid his hand on my arm. Somewhere there had been a ripple in the crowd that had reached us at last and he must steady himself. We looked at one another and he smiled. He had a bushy brown beard and a neck strong, whip-corded. His deep blue eyes were genial, but his mouth within his beard hard and fanatical. Surely he had known Savonarola, witnessed the great Bonfire of Luxury, stood sternly, perhaps, unflinchingly before that later terrible burning. I almost asked him how it had been on that day, whether he had felt pity, whether it had seemed to him that the skies had opened to receive the Saint. . . .

Roman Fountain

But there was a stir, a wind of concentration, a drawing of the breath. Pius XI had been taken from his Chapel where last night I had seen him and was being borne up the aisle to the far Altar.

It was, or seemed to me, a strange procession, for it was huddled, confused, one man pressing upon another. I could just see the figure aloft, illumined by the flickering lights, the pinched yellow face, the gold of the mitre.

A moment later the procession was close to me. My view was uninterrupted. I saw very sharply the waxed flesh into which the purple colour was now everywhere breaking, the stiff hands, the pointed shoes. All about it the crowd shuffled and hurried along. There seemed to me no reverence, but the very *odour* of the Mediaeval Age — a rich, dry, crackling odour of crusted ornateness and profitable superstition, of gaiety and cruelty, a passion for beauty, a disregard of pain, everything hot and pressed, and high-lit and dusky; above all, a sniff of immortality. Here in this hustling, coloured, untidy crowd about the courts was something that Time had not touched at all.

They turned my corner and everyone pressed forward to see what would happen next. I remember curiously little music in the whole affair.

There were dim muted Gregorians with that undertone of rasping humanity, but the music, at any rate, gave no solemnity to the proceedings.

I pressed forward with the rest, carried upwards on the enormous stomach of a crimson-robed priest who was muttering to himself and, finding me pressed upon him, sighed and groaned a little and then took it all as part of the day's ceremony. But I could see nothing. The three coffins were there, one inside another, but they were lost in the sea of pushing, struggling, staring individuals.

I went back to my steps and waited.

I had to wait a very long time indeed, for the oddest thing happened. The lead gave out for soldering the coffins. They had to send to a shop to buy some more lead! Here was the burial of the greatest Monarch in the world and they had not enough lead to solder him into his coffins. Someone ran out into the street to buy some lead as you might for a fishing-line. And inside the Basilica we all waited.

I sank into a kind of dream. I thought, I don't know why, of the time when I had known Hitler at Bayreuth in '24. He had come to Bayreuth for the Opera. We were both friends of Winnie Wagner's. He was but recently out of Munich prison and was attended by a bodyguard of young men. We had some talks though. I found his German very hard to understand, and he would have found *my* German yet more difficult had he ever listened to anything I said. I remember that he cried, and that I felt his passion for Germany so sincere that it seemed to burn through his ugly boots into the ground, and that I liked him and thought him, in every way, tenth-rate.

In that I was wrong. It was his emotional instability that struck me. I was sure that soon he would be killed and that gave him a kind of sacred dedicated air. He also thought it likely. Men have called him a coward. That, I am sure, he was not. He reminded me greatly of a medium who conducted a séance in Conan Doyle's house when I was present once. I felt that I might hear a tambourine shake and a trumpet toot at any moment when Hitler was present. I told Winnie Wagner this and she was very indignant. She said that he was to be the Saviour of the World.

But why did I think of him now? Because I could perceive already that the centre of this adventure was to be found in the genuineness, the reality of Belief. *My* Belief — the Belief of everyone concerned.

Here and now did many of the people in this

Basilica at this moment really believe that Pius XI
was now in Purgatory — as truly and surely in
Purgatory as I was now standing, pressed in on
every side, feeling the old familiar ache in my
instep, the slight stiffness of my left shoulder, the
pleasant dryness of my tongue and throat? Was I
myself sure of my own individual immortality?
Did I truly believe that this personal identity,
named for the moment Hugh Walpole, was to go
on and on, experiencing, working, hoping, loving?
Did I *believe* that as I believed that I was wearing a
white bow tie? Where was the Centre? Was I
to find it, surely, once and for all, during these
Italian weeks?

There was movement. The tide had turned.
We were pressed back and sardined together.
The coffins had at last been fastened down. No
one on this earth would ever see the face of
Pius XI again. The last turn of his journey was to
be accomplished. With Hillman and Noyes I
moved over, nearer to the Baldacchino, and there,
in front of the Altar, above the crypt into which
the body was to be lowered, towering over the
myriad trembling candles, was the Pulley.

This was a queer thing indeed set up in the
middle of all that splendour and ornate ceremony.
It was a high triangle of wood with dangling ropes,

rather like the executioner's gibbet.

If not the actual specimen, it resembled exactly the Pulley that had been used through century after century for this ceremony. It had a naked simplicity, an unadorned forthrightness that stamped reality upon the scene. The reality of history, the reality of death, the reality of the insignificance of man, the reality of the inevitability of destruction. It was mocking if you like, above the crimson of the Cardinals' robes, but it was true, simple, direct. To this, however many trumpets, candles, brocades and velvets there may be, we must in the end come.

Up to the Pulley simple unstained wooden planks were running. Against these planks, on either side, the whole crowd pressed and pushed — priests and monks, Noble Guards, Swiss Guards, choristers and choirmen, old gentlemen in evening dress, journalists and veiled ladies.

The procession was advancing. There was a halt. There was a great silence.

I noticed then that the Basilica had grown darker.

This darkening of the scene had been, I suppose, theatrically arranged by man, but it certainly seemed as though it were intended by God. So gradually had it progressed that we had noticed nothing. The music that, as I have said, had never been obtrusive, appeared now to have died away altogether. The Basilica had the gloom of an impending thunder-storm. The lights around the Baldacchino, where we all now were, flickered bravely but seemed to be blown by a mean underground wind. The Pulley, the gaunt wood, the dangling ropes, the bare boards of the platform, appeared to threaten all of us — this pushing, bustling, pressing crowd — with imminent death. In the middle of ceremony, gold, and incense, death was the one reality.

The other immediate reality was to push the three-in-one coffin up the slope, under the Pulley. Workmen appeared, strong young men in their shirt-sleeves who belonged to any kind of work that was more important than show. They wore blue working trousers, and now as they shoved at the coffin you could see their thighs and buttocks magnificently straining, and all of us in the crowd — frilled priests and evening-tie old men and fancy-ball Papal Guards — appeared over-dressed. The bodily functions were the thing — straining and pushing, filling and emptying, sweating and shivering, clutching and releasing. Get the coffin up the slope! Push it and shove it and heave at it! We've had one failure today already when we

hadn't enough lead to solder the coffins with —
don't let's have another! And, when we've done
our job — for what's a Pope but just another man?
— let's be off to our bottle of wine and pasta
and, if we're lucky, a girl to be in bed with when
the day's work's over!

The Pope was a good fellow — he climbed
mountains and liked spaghetti and took pills for
his bowels like any other — What's this? God's
Minister on earth? Well, maybe. We'll go to a
Mass if we've time. Who knows how true all
that is? But what *is* true is that this is heavy and
will roll off the boards if we're not careful and
that will be another scandal. So — heave-ho!
lads — and the young giant with the black tum-
bling hair pushes out his chest and licks his hands
while St. Peter's grows ever darker and darker
about him, and the choir-boys, the priests, the
soldiers, the journalists push against one another,
and peer and snuffle and gaze and pray, their lips
moving as violently as their eyes, for the peace of
the soul of their late Father in God, Pope Pius XI.

Up the slope the coffin slides: it is under the
ropes. Now it must be raised, lifted over the
dark gulf between the candles and lowered then
to rest, for ever (unless in a month or two a bomb
falls from the sky), in the crypt beside the other

coffins. To my surprise I discover that a large Noble Guard looking like one of the soldiers in the last act of *Tosca* (also closely resembling a friend of mine in England) is crying. The tears roll down his cheeks. He can't raise his white-gloved hands to dry them, for he is pressed in so tightly by priests and choir-boys. He stands there, motionless, his face grave and tender, the tears chasing one another. His eyes are large and wondering, like those of my dog, Ranter, when I cry out in sudden surprise. He is not in the least ashamed of his tears. I think how very, very nice the Italians are and that they are unlikely to be of very much use to the Germans.

The struggle to fix the ropes so firmly to the coffin that there can be no possible accident is breath-taking. The workmen are quite audibly cursing them on the platform above us, as in all probability they cursed four hundred years ago over precisely the same tiresome business. They bend and stretch and pull at the ropes. The coffin joggles a little, rises slightly, then settles down again. The coffin is amazingly human, even ironically obstinate. It has no sense of ceremony, only of rather ill-bred power.

Someone is pushing into my back as though they would break my body in half. I lean upon the Noble Guard, who is a rock of strength, a weeping rock of strength. I feel that we are brothers and have known one another always. I try to prevent myself from realizing that his breath smells strongly of garlic. And what is garlic after all? Is it not the colour of the country?

I hear a little dialogue behind me, American-accented.

" Well, I'll do my best to be there two-thirty."

" If I'm late don't wait. Go straight on."

" It's a bore Alice not coming."

" You know what she is. You can't depend on her."

" No, you can't. Says one thing and means another."

The coffin is rising. The ropes creak, but they have a firm manly grip on the coffin now. The young workman straightens his back and wipes his brow. There is singing all around me. The coffin is aloft, then slowly down, down it comes, level with the flickering candles, below them, out of sight.

The ropes are released.

We are in semi-darkness. It is as though night had fallen unexpectedly on us; we are lost and alone.

But the Noble Guard turns his head a little, looks at me, smiles with a great relief.

VIII

BACK in my attic bedroom again, starting to undress, I realized a moment of extreme apprehension.

I have said before in this narrative that there are times when I am sure that life is, in positive reality, a dream, and that I shall wake up any hour and find that I am back in my dormitory at R—— again, waking to that swaying and sinking of my bed, aware that in a moment I shall be thrown out of it, stripped of my nightshirt and beaten with corded towels. At such moments my apprehension is exactly the same as it was forty years ago — I am defenceless and naked in a world of hostile enemies.

This time, however, it was the sequel to the

Roman Fountain

Funeral: the darkening Basilica, the pushing, pressing crowd, the Pulley, the dangling ropes. Death was very near — not only for myself but for the whole world. It seemed to be present with me here, in this very room. I was tired. I had had, after all, scarcely any pause since I had started driving from Keswick two days ago. I was tired, excited, lonely, even home-sick.

I smiled as I put on my pyjamas to reflect how to many people I appeared self-complacent. It had begun in the old days when I wore, as I have already described, pince-nez on the end of a chain, and I would walk about with my chin in the air (and I have a prominent chin) to keep them in their place. The accusation also came from my active consciousness of happiness at the moment of its activity. To say, whether to yourself or anyone else, " Oh, how happy I at this moment, 10.45, am! " is disgusting, even obscene. I have a friend who does this and I know therefore how exasperating it is.

Two sentences also have for long confirmed my tiresome complacency. One is at the beginning of a novel of mine, *Fortitude*, now nearly thirty years old: *'Tisn't life that matters but the courage you bring to it* — and the other is something that, quite honestly but most incautiously, I said years ago to that friend who sees wrong motives in everything. I said: " If one has a person to love, a place to love, work to love, and averagely decent health, life is worth living." This platitudinous copy-book remark has been repeated again and again with derisive comments. If I had heard it and was told that So-and-so had uttered it, I also would have derided it.

And yet the longer I live the more profoundly true both of these simple remarks prove to be. If the sentence from *Fortitude* had appeared in *War and Peace* in Tolstoi's best Russian (or, better still, in one of Tchekov's most melancholy little short stories) it would be quoted as a truth, profound and ironical. Or if I had only added " My little dog likes nuts," as the Governess in *The Cherry Orchard* crosses the room remarking, I too, although I would have been accused of imitating Katherine Mansfield, would have been applauded by the sophisticated.

The trouble was that I naïvely showed that I believed what I said, and that to be naïf without irony has, quite rightly, for fifty years been considered a proof of immaturity.

But — complacent! Had I ever, in all my life, felt secure — secure of myself, my position, my

religion, my friends, my work, the world's progress? Yes, of my friends — of one at least, I
was now quite definitely secure. But of nothing
else. Life, still now at fifty-five, was like a ride
at the edge of precipices in a very rickety coach.
One was poised, quivering, above certain death.
It was foolish, but pleasant, to observe at the
same time the colour of the flowers that grew on
the banks, the superb view ahead of us, and the
lovely, exquisitely formed legs of the young lady
seated exactly opposite one.

I did not even know, I thought, as I lay down
in the bed that had been so recently a rather
dusty sofa, and arranged on the little table beside
me Symonds' *Renaissance* and the Dumas, whether
I wanted the apprehension *not* to be there! The
Pulley with its dangling ropes stood formidably in
front of me. We must all die. Everyone in that
Basilica would, in a moment, as history goes, be
a disintegrating corpse. Even now, as I turned on
my right side, there might present itself a new
little pain. A pain quite different from all the
other pains. A tiny, squeezing, whispering pain
somewhere near the navel. And I would then
turn on my left side thinking that thus I would
rid myself of it. No, it was still there. I would
fall asleep. And what an amazement to discover,

on waking in the morning, that it was yet with me! A new companion and by no means a good one.

A week or two later and I might learn that I was doomed. "It began, doctor, one night in Rome. I was as well as anything while I was undressing. I lay on my side, beginning to read . . ." Sentence has been pronounced. Walking from the doctor's consulting-room you are divided from all your fellows, from this world of cloud and sky, of food, of love, of bills and the publication of novels. Hitler and Mussolini mean nothing to you any more. The hangman's rope, the executioner's axe are not more certain.

Complacent? Any of us? I thought of B—— W——, who certainly *appears* complacent, of Mrs. S—— and the little banker in X——. We are all together, all in the same leaky boat. We may as well be friendly and show a general tolerance.

As I fell into sleep the coffin bumped, shook, raised itself, slowly fell into the abyss. I saw the tears trickling down the stout cheeks of the Noble Guard. He was crying for all of us.

IX

THAT walk up the hill to the hotel was to become something of great importance to me. In the first place it discovered for me the melancholy bittersweet tang of my old age. I was no longer as young! I had in fact three halting-places: one at the door of the shop with the glass and metal ornaments for the modern home — the steel armchair, the glass-topped table, the mirror with dead ebony border! My second stop was at the corner where the little helmeted policeman was, the corner that had the shop with the photographs of Mussolini and Ciano — Mussolini like a self-confident bull showing off before the other bulls, and Ciano with his hat so doggily raked that he seems to slant to one side, toppling over against the wind. The third stopping-place was by the flower-shop just before the last steep twist up to the Ambassadors.

These pauses were that I might recover my breath. They were also little ' signs ' towards the recovery of my Fountain — just as in a game, when you are searching for something you are given ' signs ' as to whether you are hot or cold.

The modern furniture-shop that I was to come to know so well represented that attempt on the part of modern Italy to deny the very existence of the Fountain. It was the spirit *against* the spirit of all the saffron-coloured walls, the Square with the church and the tobacco-shop, the Spanish Steps, the light over Rome from the Janiculum, the ' Pietà ' in St. Peter's . . . and it failed. It failed utterly. However cheap, mechanical, hideous, the modern creative spirit in the art of living may be, you may see in Paris and New York at least what is intended. In all Italy it is a failure, just as the statues in the Foro Mussolini are failures. Italy refuses to lead the modern life creatively. Creation is still in the vines and the olives, in the oxen and the goats, in the pale sunlight that caresses the castle wall, in the long rustle of the sea across the beaches of Paestum. But in this furniture-shop, no! The dust is even now blowing about the steel armchair, and the pale disharmony of the glassy mirror is stained with dead flies.

Leaving the furniture-shop I pant upwards again (where are my morning exercises once gallantly stiffened with an oath to eternity?) and reach the window of Mussolini and Ciano. I have passed, as it were, triumphantly, the first attempt towards the disavowal of my Fountain. I reach the second: the presentation of the armed might of the new Imperial Italy. I am always tempted to linger here, for it is at this point that the little helmeted policeman turns back the pedestrians who try to slip past him down the street.

My attention is divided between Mussolini and Ciano in the window and the little policeman. Why are they all three — Mussolini, Ciano, the little policeman — slightly ridiculous? I must not allow myself this luxury. It is so easy to make the mistake of Mr. John Garside (who is Mr. John Garside? you shall know in a minute) and consider that, because different gestures are made — I slip my shirt over my head one way, you slip your trousers down another — therefore danger is laughed out of sight. It is a case here of one chin and two headpieces. I am secure there? Don't be too sure. At this very moment the pigeon from the roof-top may have made your own unconscious dignity a mockery.

Nevertheless I move on up the hill, shaking this second menace from my shoulders. The Fountain's dancing waters are more durable than the matted chest Mussolini delights to display at hay-making time. They shine in the sun for ever, while the yellow worms feast between the strong ribs and the strutting chin is a scarecrow's helmet.

And at my third halt I am safe again. It may be that up the steps, first turn to the left, just behind the flower-shop, is the square with the Fountain. A likely place. As soon as there is time I must go and have a look.

There are always light and colour here even when it is raining. The pots of lilies, carnations, roses, camellias, are arranged in rows outside the shop. The leaves are always glistening with water, for if it is a drought there is the watering-pot, and if it rains it rains. Here there is no prison of nationality, no threat of war, no cruelty of man to man, no apprehension at the heart. On one side there is the ladies' hairdresser, on the other the hat-shop with the wisp of purple silk on one pole and a bunch of violets and a fragment of lace on the other.

Pausing here, before my last climb, looking

greedily at the white heavy languor of the camellia flowers, I think always of the three spots on earth most dear to me — Brackenburn in Cumberland, the Precincts at Canterbury, and Tregarthen's Hotel window, looking out to sea in the Scilly Isles. These three places have each a moment especially significant: at Brackenburn when the last light falls across the lawn, the Lake is grey like steel and the sloping hill above the house cuts the blue evening sky; at Canterbury when the many-coloured gardens burn on a June afternoon against the walls of the Cathedral; at the Scillies when, after a sweeping rainstorm, the sun snatches at the water and floods it, in a moment, with purple and green.

We are secure from wars and all mortal changes there far up the hill. We are safe. We are secure. The steel chairs and the photographs of heroes and the marching of the Blackshirts under the Colosseum, all, all are below us and we need no longer be afraid.

X

GOING up in the lift to my room I found on this occasion a large impressive gentleman as my companion. I saw at once that he was English. This was so beyond question that, for the moment, one could consider nothing else.

And yet it was un-English of him at once to nod, smile and say " Showery."

" Yes," I answered.

" It's my conviction that the English climate is the best in the world."

The lift-boy (the very small one with black hair and eyes like black buttons) was staring with all his might and breathing through his Roman nose. Two Englishmen in the lift at one time, and two such large ones!

"Well, I don't quite know about that!" I returned. "We don't get enough sun. That's the trouble!"

(How I was longing for my room, to shut myself in, to sink upon the bed-sofa, to reach out my hand for the heavy red *Renaissance* . . .)

The lift stopped. We got out together. The Englishman stayed at my side. He was tall and broad, dressed in a suit of dark blue that he might be wearing for the first time, so fresh was it. His white collar gleamed. In his blue tie was a pearl stud. He possessed the round and rosy countenance of an amiable baby, but his eyes were sharp, his mouth firmly set, and he had that nose so peculiarly English, strong and fleshy and almost ostentatiously nude. His hair was iron-grey and he carried over his arm an excellent waterproof.

He walked beside me and, at my door, he paused.

"You're English, of course," he said. "One could see at a glance."

I grinned foolishly.

"I hope you don't mind my speaking to you. It isn't quite the thing, of course, but the fact is that after being with foreigners all day it's pleasant to meet one of one's own people."

From nothing but cowardice I was forced to say:

" Have you been in Rome long? "

He was delighted. He beamed his pleasure.

" Several weeks. I am here on business." Then, dropping his voice a little, he said: " Rum people, the Italians."

I nodded, more cowardly than ever.

He drew closer. " You never know who's listening. Spies all over the place."

I opened my door. He stood in the doorway still beaming.

" Anyway I can say for them that their sanitation is improved since I was in Rome last. Mussolini's done that for them."

I moved forward. He stepped after me. I could see at once that he thought it very peculiar of me to have pictures, books. He looked at the coloured print of Michael Angelo's *Adam* with attention.

" You *have* made it homely."

" I like to have a few things . . ." I began.

He sighed a friendly sigh.

" Wish I had time for reading. . . ." He sighed again. " Don't you get a bit home-sick? "

" Sometimes," I said. " That's why I have these few things. . . ."

"Exactly. A foreign country's never the same thing. That's what all this trouble is about. If only foreigners would understand that we are worth two of them. Of course you can't expect them to, in a way. What they ought to see is that we've been running the world for a damned long time, and as long as we do, everything's all right. All this trouble is simply that they think we don't know what's good for them. It's the same in business. I say to them — 'That's not the way we do things in England.' "

"And what do they say?" I asked.

"Oh, they begin to argue. They are terrible fellows for talking, these Italians. Jabber, jabber. I just wait till they've stopped. They used to be all right here, but Mussolini's given them all sorts of ideas. Just because they downed a lot of natives with poison gas they think they've got an Empire. You don't think there'll be a war, do you?"

"Nobody knows."

"Exactly. You're right." He sighed again. "The worst of it is it's playing the devil with business, all this uncertainty. . . . Well, I must be getting along." He paused at sight of a photograph. "Married?"

"No, I'm a bachelor."

" Ah, that's a pity.   My wife's a brick.   Don't know what I should have done without her.   And we've got three splendid girls.   Like to see them? "

" Thanks very much."

He produced a rich pocket-book of dark leather with gold corners.   From this he abstracted a photograph of three girls sitting on a seat beside a tennis-court.   They were holding tennis racquets.

" There they are.   Margaret, Lucy and Jean. That's Jean — the small one.   Margaret's got quite a voice.   Of course it's early days yet, but I intend to give her every chance.   I call her my little Nightingale.   Jean's the tom-boy.   Up to every kind of mischief.   This is my wife."

He produced another photograph of a massive lady with pince-nez.

" Well, I must be getting along.   I hope I haven't butted in."

" Not a bit.   Not a bit."

" That's right.   I could see you wouldn't mind."

He produced a card.

" That's my name.   Garside.   We've got a lovely little place at Henley.   Any time you're that way—— "

" My name's Walpole.   I'm afraid I haven't a card."

" Walpole.   Seem to know the name somehow.
Wasn't there a writer or a painter——? "

" Yes.   Horace Walpole.   In the eighteenth
century.   He wrote letters."

" Ah, yes.   Of course.   Well, thanks awfully.
I'm in Room Ninety-two along the passage."   He
took another look at the *Adam*, said " So long,
old chap " and departed.

I liked him.   I was glad that he was gone,
though.   The room wasn't mine while he was in
it.   I lay on my sofa, stretched out my hand for
the *Renaissance*.   But it was *The Forty-five Guardsmen* that I began to read.

XI

NEXT day I went to church with Mussolini. That is how I began my article afterwards for Hillman: "Today I have been to church with Mussolini". Not that *he* cared. But I cared very much. We both worshipped together for a little while — I one thing, he quite another.

I was dressed in my ridiculous evening clothes again, and in the daylight they were shabby. I like evening clothes to be a *little* worn, or rather I dislike the armour-plated gleaming 'Tuxedo' that the American men wear. But there is shabbiness and shabbiness, and the Roman sun this morning made me like a second-house comedian in Weymouth or Plymouth who is so weary of keeping plates on the spin that he dreams of blondes upside-down while he is doing his clever trick.

Michael, who accompanied me, didn't look real either. He was grinning all over, wearing his high-shouldered, low-reaching overcoat and carrying his grey gloves. He was unreal in all his movements: his grin, his prancing walk, the swing of his coat, but he was altogether real in his cleverness with people, his kindness of heart, his generosity about anything that he possessed, the trouble that he would take to help people. What he lacked — I should imagine but don't truly know — was any kind of ambition or place in life.

He lived from moment to moment, like a brilliant little mail-coated animal who may be absorbed into the sun at any second. I always was ready to turn, after talking to someone else, and find Michael gone and only the grey gloves lying, warm and friendly, at my feet.

Today, however, as we walked along, it was Michael's aim and end to persuade me of the greatness of the Fascist power and the growing splendour of the Italians. Although he was himself an Albanian, that was, as history on the approaching Good Friday was to emphasize to us, almost the same as being an Italian. Michael reminded me in some ways of Lykiadopoulos, the

Roman Fountain

Greek Secretary to the Art Theatre in Moscow in 1914. I can see Lyki now, as, occupying the policeman's seat at the theatre, I saw, for the first time, *The Cherry Orchard* with Knipper and Kochaloff and Stanislavsky — Lyki, his sharp brilliant eyes watching me with excited eagerness to see that I was sufficiently staggered.

So Michael now. Mussolini was the greatest of men and also the most human. Michael had seen him naked when bathing — what a chest, what thighs, what a wonderful swimmer! And he had seen him with little children, he had seen him . . .

"Yes, but what does the ordinary Italian man-in-the-street think about it?"

"The ordinary Italian? Oh, he doesn't want a war with the English. Whatever the English do, however stupid they are, Sanctions or anything else, he feels friendly to the English. But the French — that's another matter. He doesn't hate the French — he doesn't hate anybody — but he thinks the French owe him something. He was treated badly after Versailles. Meanly. He'll get back what the French owe him, come what may. And the Italians feel they are great people now. Don't forget that. First-class Power, as they were in the old Roman days."

"But there's no Roman blood in the Italians any more."

"Maybe not. But they are proud all the same. They are Imperialists. They must have the Mediterranean. It is their right."

"What about the French and the English?"

"It's an Italian Sea. The French and English must recognize that. Mussolini's changed everything."

But politics, politics, politics! This book has nothing whatever to do with them. By the time that it is published — if it ever is — all these politics will have changed. A war, a death, an assassination — anything may have made, in six months, the politics on this page as stale as the sheet of newspaper that wraps my Diary in my little brown suitcase.

But not this service offered up by the Fascist State to the dead Pope. *That* is not ephemeral. It is concerned with the very roots of the Tree of Life. This very morning I have been reading in one of the books that I love most:

The open hills were airy and clear, and the remote atmosphere appeared, as it often appears on a fine winter day, in distinct planes of illumination independently toned, the rays which lit the nearer tracts of landscape streaming visibly across those further off;

a stratum of ensaffroned light was imposed on a stratum of deep blue, and behind these lay still remoter scenes wrapped in frigid grey.

It was, oddly enough, of Egdon Heath that I was thinking as I entered that baroque, over-decorated ugly church, and standing on the steps above the Square fringed with the crowd waiting to see Mussolini arrive, I saw that ' stratum of deep blue ' and the ' remoter scenes wrapped in frigid grey '. For the figure of Pius was vivid to me, striding up the mountain, his simple countenance lit with his happiness; and now the Fascist State, altogether unaware of the ' remoter scenes wrapped in frigid grey ', had gathered to salute him.

The late Pope was aware of those ' scenes '. He was host to his guests this morning and he had the advantage over them in a ' longer view '.

At the same time one practical question disturbed me. Why was I permitted to pass into the church without even a questioning glance in my direction? Nay, more than that. I was permitted to sit where I pleased. It was not that Michael's presence was sufficient excuse for me. Michael had for the moment become separated from me. But here was I, a foreigner, allowed to penetrate a building into which Mussolini would shortly enter, move as I pleased, sit where I pleased. I was not searched for weapons. I might have bomb or pistol. I could, with the greatest of ease, within the next half-hour, create history, be a man remembered for all time, change the history of the world. And the Italians didn't care.

Childishly this reassured me. It was as though I had expected a rude reception but was treated as one of the family. It was almost as though Mussolini himself had said: " Oh, let him come in! *He* won't do any harm! "

So I moved about freely and at last settled myself in a seat not far from the choir. I looked about me and realized that I was at a Party. The sensation was the Party-sensation — that of looking about you and wondering if anyone would be rude, but especially a taking-in and considering of all the Fancy Dress. One knows instinctively that it is *now* that one must catch the impression, for in another ten minutes it will be all too easily familiar and Charles I, the Red Cardinal, Pagliaccio and the White Rabbit from *Alice* will mean nothing at all. So it was now. Everyone was dressed up. The men wore gold and silver, purple and crimson; there were feathers in the hats they carried, spurs clicked at their heels, their high

collars were stiff with braid, their chests tingling
with medals. It was not a church of great size,
or at least it seemed not this morning, and so here
we all were, packed tightly together in our gold
and stiffness, with ladies in black mantillas scat-
tered among us, and all of us chattering like birds
in an aviary or the starlings on Savoy Hill.

Then I saw the catafalque, gorgeous in the
middle nave, heavy with gold, the candles burning
fiercely. Above us and around us and pressing in
upon us was the hideous decorated, twisted,
exaggerated church. It may have possessed, for
all I know, some of the most wonderful pictures
in Rome. I saw none. I saw only between the
purple hangings and above the painted Madonnas
holding bunches of paper flowers those paintings
that are surely the dreariest in the world —
prophets and priests under a dark-red sky, tortured
and triumphant, or sleepy with the exigencies of
their duties, or pompous with the consciousness of
their position. On a day it might be, wandering
idly, pushing aside the heavy leathern door, seeing
only some flickering candles and a woman praying,
reality would be there, but now, all of us dressed
like imbeciles and packed like herrings, there was
another game to be played.

Hush! It was beginning. Twilight falls on

Savoy Hill and the starlings are silent. The late Pope's principal guests have arrived. They came in, huddled and as though they were trying to escape from somebody. I detected the King, the Queen, Ciano. They all pressed to the left side of the choir, seated themselves, but still preserved that sheep-in-a-scurry confusion as though the Dog with the Fiery Eyes was after them.

And so he was! A moment later Mussolini appeared quite alone, on the right side of the choir, and sat down in a chair settled all by itself in a little peaceful place in front of the choir.

From that moment to the end, so far as the audience was concerned, he was the solitary shining point of interest. The late Pope was late indeed, and as to the poor King and Queen no one gave them a single thought. Decorum was forgotten. Ladies stood up and stared and chattered and looked at him through opera-glasses.

The very priests and prophets seemed to turn their heads in his direction.

I had never seen him before this morning and I realized that he was, for me, another ' sign ' pointing towards my discovery of the Fountain. Physically he was very simple indeed. He was dressed in the plainest of uniforms, his bald head shone in the candlelight, his chin jutted out. When he stood up on this occasion or that he was a little squat broad-shouldered man with thick legs and a naked head. When he sat down the chin jutted upwards and upwards as though it were searching for something or were offering some ruffian the incredible opportunity to launch his fist at it.

But — what would I have felt on the first vision of Alexander, Hannibal, Caesar, Napoleon? Would I have shivered at the back of my neck? Would my veins have turned to water? Hannibal in the Alps, Caesar as he fell in the senate house, Napoleon at St. Helena? And Mussolini — where? I don't know. I am unable to suggest. Not marching on Rome, not directing his legions towards Abyssinia, not riding his white horse in Africa. In all these there is, for some reason, a suggestion of the ludicrous.

Here he was not ludicrous, but not wonderful either. My feeling towards him was friendly and even protective. He seemed to me so very ordinary a man. He was not that, of course, but he was most certainly ageing; his eyes closed once or twice, it seemed to me, with a gesture of infinite weariness — or was it boredom?

His loneliness, my romantic imagination was, in all probability, licking its lying lips over. Are not all great men lonely? We are always told so, no doubt for the consolation of our lesser personalities. But this was not the loneliness of a great man. It was the loneliness of a lonely man, who is lonely, as we all are lonely, because he is not quite certain of his safety, nor sure as to his destiny.

While seated he never moved and perhaps was thinking profoundly. I imagined rather that he was not thinking at all and had done very little thinking for a considerable time past. The thinking he left now to his daughter and his son-in-law.

He never looked to right or left of him, and yet he must have been well aware that at any moment the bomb might be thrown or the revolver fired. For the first time I speculated as to whether the real reason of his safety was — that he was not important any more. And if *he* were not important, most certainly the huddled Royalties on the other side of the choir were even less important.

I felt a temptation to rise like Alice and shout: " Why, they are only a pack of cards after all! "

And yet I knew well enough all the danger that there was here — danger to myself, danger to all the present world. Where then did the danger lie?

And then quite unexpectedly, as though it were the Pope himself, with a friendly brotherly gesture, pulling me back to the only thing that mattered here, I was conscious of the choir. They were singing the *Dies Irae*, that terrible warning, with the shrill high note that the Roman Catholics have, something altogether sexless and with passion of only a spiritual sort. Day of Wrath! Day of Wrath! It was impossible to glance round at these uniforms, this blaze of gold and purple, and feel that anything but a material day of wrath was contemplated by anybody.

I knew nevertheless that we were all in the same boat — Mussolini, the King, Ciano — that the remaining years for all of us were very few, and that yet only a few of us were giving death a thought. Mussolini himself must have considered it many times. Was he a coward or a brave man? There were stories that confirmed either opinion. But now, at such a service as this, paying his respects to that simple, courageous man, was there any consideration of God in his mind? Was there any consideration of God in my own?

I knew then, at that instant, why it was that I had come to that service. It was precisely as though Pius' firm country hand was on my shoulder and he said to me: "Before you go further in all this, my brother, you must make a clear statement. Sign this paper before you move into the next room."

I was caught up as was Browning's man in *Christmas Eve*. Such moments come, of course, to all of us, when everything rolls away like a Japanese house-wall and we are amazed at the landscape we see. It has been there all the time. Why have we not realized it?

I presented, looking into the candles of the catafalque, my three reasons of Faith — commonplace platitudinous ones, offered by many a poor unphilosophical creature like myself many many times. But they were my own, won by my life's experience. I could go by no other evidence offered by however great a Saint, wise a philosopher, scornful an atheist. I knew only my own heart and this was the story of it.

First the personality and character of Jesus Christ Himself. I had read that He had never existed. Georg Brandes, whom I had known once in Denmark, had written a book to prove it. I had been told and had read again and again that there was nothing new in His doctrine, that He was a commonplace obscure rebel, that His Divinity was a myth. I didn't know about His Divinity, but I did know that, increasingly through my life,

had I never been told a word about Him and had
chanced upon the Lord's Prayer, the Sermon on
the Mount, the sayings and the Parables, His
tenderness to little children and all the lost, His
anger and indignation, the details of the Last
Supper and the Crucifixion, I would have cried
out: " Here is a Man like no other man who has
ever been, and in realizing Him I go beyond all
earthly physical things into the world of the Spirit.
If He is true then the life of the Spirit is true."

And secondly — for my time is short, the *Dies
Irae* is closing, soon, soon all will be ended — my
love for my friends. They are, I suppose, ordinary
human beings as I myself am ordinary. There are
many millions like us. As I tell Pius the names
of the people I love — David, Athene, George,
Ellie, Alan, Jo, Harold, Ethel, Owen, Ronald,
Dorothy, Rose, Jim, Chug, John, Jack, Robin,
Jean — and there are more, but I have very little
time — I know that they are very ordinary names.
" But that, Pius, is why I repeat them to you.
Seen from an aeroplane they would be like flies.
Passed in the street they would be part of the
great flood of humanity. Because I love them I
know them and because I know them I discover
qualities of courage, unselfishness, gaiety, patience
in suffering that penetrate so deeply into their

natures that they go beyond all physical qualities. Beyond their bodies they live, but I only know this because I love them. And I think, Pius, that love can discover anything and belongs to what we call the soul.

"And thirdly, Pius, my friend — for now you *are* my friend. A little while ago I might only kiss your ring — now I am with you and you are with me for ever. Thirdly I am aware in my own experience of a spiritual life as active as my physical life. You may say, my scornful acquaintance, writing poems in London, that that is wish-fulfilment, and part of my romantic, sentimental nature. Yes, it is part of me. That is true. But I can judge only by my own experience. I have not wished to be aware of this other life. Often I have fought it, for it is troublesome and interfering, betraying my complacency, taking all pleasure from earthly achievement, interfering with my pleasant views but sometimes oddly reaching me through them. Oh, Pius, Pius, all this is too hard for me. Pray for me where you are! Shelter me a little when I am in great darkness! Be with me in my loneliness."

Everyone is on the move. Mussolini is standing, alone, short, squat, chin in air. He is gone.

Roman Fountain

It is farewell to Pius, the good mountaineer.
No one will think of him any more — or only a
very few. His sister, his nephew, a friend or two
— one friend whom I myself will shortly know.
But this service has closed him down, surrendered
him truly to the earth. He belongs to an already
forgotten history, and at once, even as we move
out of the church, we are discussing the question
of his successor.

XII

IN the morning I found it was true. Everyone had turned his face from the dead Pope. Everyone was looking, as he might in the Derby of the clerical year, to the possible winner of the Election Stakes. And on the morning after that again I discovered further.

My telephone rang, and lounging in my bed I answered it. It was Hillman. With that temperate calm kindliness so especially his, he told me that my article of the evening before 'wouldn't do'.

"Won't do? Why not?"

"It's too political."

"Too political? But it isn't political at all."

"Quite. But in New York they think it is. Here,

I have a cable: ' Walpole's article too political '. "

His calmness infuriated me. I was suddenly submerged with one of those waves of passionate anger that are altogether childish, absurd and futile. I am fifty-five years of age and I have not yet outgrown them. I have not yet outgrown them because they catch me so unexpectedly. I am at peace. I am all amiability. Like Heine in the *Harzreise*, ' Today is the first of May . . . my love is bursting the bud, and is shooting up in lyric flashes, in immortal dithyrambs, in ebullience of song '. (Dreadful translation by Francis Storr!) And then — there is a chance word, a movement, a smile, and the blood has burst in my head like fireworks on the Fifth of November. I see nothing, hear nothing, feel nothing but a passionate flaming desire to destroy my enemy. Words pour from me. I say anything, lies, curses, accusations, insinuations, anything, anything, however rash and scandalous. A moment later it is all over and I am nothing but a fool, regretting a thousand things. Surely, surely, at *my* age? If only they were not so sudden, so unexpected, if they would but give me a little warning. Last year — how many were there? Only three. And this year, 1939, so far only two. But we are in July. There is yet a long time to go.

Roman Fountain

So now, lying on my stomach, I shouted down the telephone at Hillman. Political? Who dared say they were political? He himself had complimented me on my articles. Had he not? (" Certainly, certainly," murmured Hillman.) Well, then, would he have complimented me had I been political? He had warned me from the very beginning *not* to be political. I had obeyed orders. I had *not* been political. (" Nevertheless," murmured Hillman with that American quiescence that comes, they say, from the Indians, " in New York they think that. . . ."

Now indeed was my head all Roman candles and spluttering Catherine-wheels. They thought that in New York, did they? Did Hillman know, then, what they could do in New York? And did he know, also, what *I* would do? I would straightway return to London — oh yes, by the very next train or plane or whatever was quickest or soonest. I would break my contract. They could do in New York what they jolly well pleased. (I announced this breaking of my contract as though it were of world importance, as though the complete Hearst organization would be smashed by it.) Hillman only murmured, " Oh yes. . . . See you in the office at eleven," and rang off.

I lay muttering on my bed, and suddenly perceiving the friendly, encouraging fingers of God the Father extended to Adam as visioned by the gnarled but reverent spirit of Michael Angelo, I felt the fool that I had been.

I went down to the office very quietly, rather as Anne in *Persuasion* approaches Captain Wentworth on a country walk. I entered first the lavatory to settle my wits and looked across to the barber-shop, and down into the Colonnades. Then, humbly gentle before the kindly Hillman, I discovered a yet worse thing — that to fulfil my contract, between now and the Election I must write an article for the American public every single day and that that article must be concerned, in one way or another, with Papal affairs.

" But I didn't contract to do that."

" I think that you did."

" I contracted only to write about the Funeral and the Coronation."

" To write every day *between* the Funeral and the Coronation."

" And that may be how long? "

" Three weeks very probably. Today is February 23rd. The Cardinals from abroad will not arrive much before March 1st. I should say that the Coronation will be around the 12th."

" And I have to write an article *every* day? "

" It won't be so bad.   We'll help you."

" But I can't write articles about *nothing* at all."

" That's what journalists have continually to be doing."

With what loathing I looked round me upon those two ugly little sinister rooms.   Here was my torture-chamber!   Here I must shout into Hillman's typewriter every single day of three long weeks fifteen hundred words about nothing at all. Then I looked upon Hillman and loved him.   For he understood everything that was in my mind. He was as father to child.   He hoped, oh, so truly he hoped that I wouldn't be a completely bloody fool!

So I said: " This day one hundred and eighteen years ago Keats died.   I'm going with Noyes to see his grave."

Noyes, it must be remembered, was in exactly the same position as myself.   He too must write an article every day.   And surely it was worse for Noyes because he was a poet.   But Alfred was older in spirit than I.   He had learnt control and the proper proportion of things.   He had been married twice and had children.   His book on Voltaire had been censored by his own Church because, so far as I could see, he had tried very hard to prove that Voltaire was a Christian. He was calm and kindly and generous, and listened to my prattlings as though he were one of his own very human saints.

We drove out to Keats' grave together. As we went along we discussed the desperate vanities of others.

" The fiery particle snuffed out——— "

" *Not* by the article. Keats was killed neither by criticism nor by Fanny Brawne. He was killed by consumption, physical disease and physical disease alone. There is nothing worse than the harm that physical disease can do to the soul. Look at Keats before that fatal walking-tour — his brightness, his gaiety, the way that he brushed all his troubles aside. Then Tom's death and the beginning of the disease in himself. . . . As though he cared a rap at abuse of *Endymion*. When he was in health he had a vision far beyond that immediate moment. The disease narrowed the physical vision until it concentrated at last to — ' the silk lining she put in my travelling cap scalds my head '. If he had been in health do you imagine that he wouldn't have seen Fanny Brawne as she was, a vain, light-minded little flirt? And do you blame her? Was it amusing for a pretty common young girl to be engaged to a poet dying of consumption, whose poems the papers laughed at? Keats *well*, ambitious, amusing, handsome, although he *was* so short of stature, was one thing; little, consumptive, penniless, sick-faced Keats quite another. I don't blame Miss Brawne but I can't abide her. My only comfort in Keats' death is that she would have made Keats miserable had he been in health and married her."

"I don't agree with you about Fanny Brawne. Those letters written to Keats' sister, published two years ago, showed her to be a woman of sense and courage and tenderness."

"Not in the least. She was kind, of course, and by the time she wrote to Fanny she had realized that he *was* somebody after all. She had a good light heart and was thoroughly common and vulgar."

We were at the Protestant Cemetery, a place that I have always greatly disliked. Not here, not here was any Fountain, but rather the ugly tomb of Caius Cestius that will outlast everything of loveliness and charm, the pressed, packed graves, the darkness of the overhanging trees. Here is Keats' grave with no name at the head of it, and Severn's, and Shelley's heart, and his little son William.

Noyes and I picked leaves from the violet

plants. Someone sneezed close beside me, but I could see no one. It seemed that the tomb of Caius Cestius was about to open.

"Come away! Come away, Alfred! There are ghosts."

But he preferred to walk among the graves. We discussed friendship and whether Severn had not bored Keats to anguish. But I returned for a moment to Severn's grave.

"He was a good man — and he had the luck of the devil."

But what was poetry? What was *great* poetry? Alfred, who can quote anything, repeated:

> " *As when upon a tranced summer-night*
> *Forests, branch-charmed by the earnest stars,*
> *Dream, and so dream all night without a noise.*
> *Save from one gradual solitary gust*
> *Swelling upon the silence, dying off*
> *As if the ebbing air had but one wave,*
> *So came these words and went; the while in tears*
> *She prest her fair large forehead to the earth,*
> *Just where her fallen hair might spread in curls*
> *A soft and silken net for Saturn's feet.*
> *Long, long these two were postured motionless,*
> *Like sculpture builded-up upon the grave*
> *Of their own power.*"

I replied with:

Roman Fountain

" *Among these turf-stacks graze no iron horses*
   Such as stalk, such as champ in towns and the soul of
      crowds,
   Here is no mass-production of neat thoughts,
   No canvas shrouds for the mind nor any black hearses:
   The peasant shambles on his boots like hooves
   Without thinking at all or wanting to run in grooves."

" Good heavens! What's that? "

" The only piece of modern verse I can remember. Louis MacNeice. My favourite after
Eliot of modern poets. You are *not* a modern
poet, Alfred."

" Certainly not. What was that? ' The
peasant shambles——' "

" *The peasant shambles on his boots like hooves*
   Without thinking at all or wanting to run in grooves."

" But the metre—— "

" This is sprung verse and you can run as many
syllables into a line as you please."

" Yes, but—— "

" All the same I believe that what determines
great poetry is how far down it goes:

     Woman! when I behold thee flippant, vain,
     Inconstant, childish, proud and full of fancies;
     Without that modest softening that enhances
     The downcast eye, repentant of the pain

That its mild light creates to heal again;
E'en then, elate, my spirit leaps and prances,
E'en then my soul with exultation dances. . . .

That hasn't much depth, has it? That's pretty awful, isn't it?"

"Of course."

"It's Keats all the same. But

Dying off
As if the ebbing air had but one wave

isn't that of an unfathomable depth, timeless, independent of all circumstance, schools, fashions, years, sicknesses, quarrels? MacNeice hasn't been touched as yet by *that* divinity . . . nor any younger poet in England. Perhaps we curse our own time too much, are hysterical about what may happen to us — as though it mattered in comparison with—— "

"Keats didn't want to die."

"He is more alive now than then."

"Do you think that's any comfort to a man? Actually he had the torture of frustrated love, and consuming fevers, and cheated ambition. Even though he knows now that the water in which his name was written is a living stream — hasn't he other things much more important to think about? He and Byron and Shelley as they work, singing, at the New Jerusalem have little memory of Williams and the foundering boat, of the silk lining to the travelling cap, of the club foot and tiresome Caroline Lamb — and we, we who are here, we make so much of them."

"Perhaps the departed Pope has just joined them. . . . Keats would like him. . . . Alfred, someone *did* sneeze by the grave. I have my violet leaf."

We were in the town again and soon I was climbing the Pincian.

XIII

IT had not really needed Hillman and the article-a-day discovery to show me that I was now in the middle period of my adventure. For a fortnight — probably for three weeks — very little would happen in the Papal world. The Cardinals would be arriving from distant places; all the intrigues, both inside the Vatican and outside, would be developing. Already the kiosks showed the illustrated papers open at the double-page photographs of all the Cardinals. Over sixty of them! And seen thus, like masks, without any personal knowledge of them, you could divide them into the Spiritual, the Worldly, the Fleshly without very much difficulty. How dreadfully our faces betray us, especially eyes and mouth! Some of the

Cardinals looked like goats and satyrs, some like
sharp little country-town lawyers, some like actors
very conscious of their parts; one or two
were noble.

" What's he like? " I asked Michael, pointing.

" That's Pacelli, secretary to the late Pope.
That's why he won't be elected. They never elect
a secretary, because they want someone with a new
policy. It's a pity, because he's a grand man."

I looked at those burning eyes, those sharp,
tense but kindly lips. I felt as though I had known
him a long time.

" That's the man for me," I said.

But I saw that for a fortnight now I must make
my own life. I was very much alone. Tom
Driberg, whom I had immensely liked, had gone
back to London, Noyes was married, the Americans had their constant preoccupying journalism.
I did not mind being alone at all. I was delighted.
I had much to see, much to read. Now was the
excellent time for my Fountain.

I would like to repeat here that this business
about the Fountain was most truly neither whimsy
nor affectation. It simply was that, thirty years
before, I had stumbled upon something most
beautiful, and had known a moment of ecstatic
experience when, as in a dream or under an

anaesthetic, everything seems to be made plain. It was that moment of experience, of revelation that I would recover. Three-quarters of my life was over, and now always, beneath my daily affairs, was this preoccupation with the puzzle of existence. I should never solve it. That was certain. But I must pursue continually all the clues. I was never left alone for a moment. The Hound of Heaven had me in his charge. In fact, put quite simply, here was a most beautiful thing that I had once seen. I wanted to see it again.

By now Rome had delivered itself geographically to me. I knew where everything was. I was surprised at its smallness — thirty years ago it had seemed a wilderness. Down the Umberto, past my office Piazza and Marcus Aurelius, straight on to the Victor Emmanuel Monument, the Forum, the Colosseum, the Capitol — all the clustered beehive old Roman world. Then in the other direction down the Corso, past my restaurant, out to the Piazza del Popolo, past the hotel where lived the Noyes. To the right of the Corso you might branch off at any turn you wished and so to the Spanish Steps, and the flowers and Keats' house and the Via del Babuino with the curiosity shops. Beyond the river Castel St. Angelo and St. Peter's. Above my hotel, on the Pincian, the

Roman Fountain

Borghese Gardens. Above the Victor Emmanuel Monument the Terminus Station, the Diocletian Baths with the gallery. There, roughly, was the whole of my Rome, the Rome that I now came to love with a deep and abiding passion.

Somewhere inside that Rome was my Fountain. I consulted my guide-book.

FOUNTAINS

Barberini	Of Piazza Popolo
Barcaceia	Of the River Gods
Of Moses	Of St. Peter's
Of the Najades	Of Tortoises
Pauline	Of Trevi

Of the Triton

Only three of these were possible. I looked up ' Of the Najades '. I read: ' The large picturesque fountain in the centre, is a modern work by Guerrieri (1885) '. *That* wasn't mine, then.

I looked ' Of the River Gods '. I read: ' The square is beautifully decorated by three fountains, the one in the centre, by Bernini, is composed of four rocks supporting a pedestal on the top of which is an obelisk found in the Circus of Romulus in the Appian Way '. I knew that one. *That* wasn't my Fountain.

I looked up ' Of the Triton '. I read: ' The fountain in the centre of the square represents a

Triton on the sea shell, throwing out a jet of water. It is the work of Bernini, executed for Pope Urban VIII in 1640.' *That* was not my Fountain.

No, it was clear that, in the tourist sense, my Fountain was of very little importance. It was not chronicled at all. I was rather glad to know this. I felt that the Fountain belonged all the more to myself — or rather to Mr. Montmorency, for it was he who had found it for me.

His personality — the bald head with wisps of hair, the dirty finger-nails, the dampness, the eagerness, the furtiveness — came back to me again so that it was almost as though he were at my side. Was he alive still, or was it his ghost who now accompanied me? Thirty years was a long time for a weak flabby physique such as his. Had he died? If so, where? In some shabby Roman lodging, or, like Corvo, pimping for the perverted taste of rich elderly gentlemen in Venice or Naples? Was he not perhaps yet here, in Rome, and might I not enter some little restaurant one evening to find him seated there, greedily waiting to share my spaghetti? He would not find this time, alas, as simple, naïf, single-hearted a child as he found then — and yet I would follow him now just as I followed him then, that shabby, soiled Pied Piper who knew the way to the Beautiful Country.

Every day, then, for the next fortnight I prosecuted a little my search. I had a notion that the hidden Square must be between the Victor Emmanuel Monument, the Pantheon, the Spanish Steps and the Quirinal, thus:

Spanish Steps

Quirinal

*

Pantheon

Victor Emmanuel

I came to know many of the little streets in this quarter exceedingly well — the Via delle Muratte, the Coppelle, the Rondanini, the Via Frattina, the Via del Seminario at the back of the Pantheon, the Via dei Prefetti — and so on and so on. The trouble was that all these little streets were so exactly alike, narrow and smelling of cats and pasta and an odd scent compounded of snuff, incense and the unwashen parts of the human person. In almost all of them there was a wall of burnt umber, a shop with pasta, a shop with cheap tinkling ornaments, a restaurant with a piece of veal and a cabbage in the window, a shop with coloured postcards and packets of yellow-looking envelopes, a shop with delicious Stevensonian cream puffs and chocolate cakes, a

sudden vista of a square or a church with steps
and a black leathern-aproned door. Hidden somewhere among all of these — hidden, hidden,
hidden — was my Fountain.

Once only, in that fortnight, I thought I had
come upon it. I had passed a dingy little
stationer's in whose window was a shabby collection of second-hand English books and among the
books a faded green-and-gold Matthew Arnold.
Standing there I was suddenly caught back into
two scenes one behind the other. One was of a
blazing summer day in the Scillies when Harold
and myself were lazing on Tresco — the beach
immediately below Cromwell's Castle.

I had taken with me my Oxford India-paper
Matthew Arnold and Miss Braddon's *John March-
mont's Legacy* in its old yellowback. (Why is
the whole of Miss Braddon's magnificent ' œuvre '
out of print? *Why*, when a modern thriller will
sell its fifty thousand, are *Lady Audley*, *Aurora
Floyd*, *Henry Dunbar*, *The Fatal Three*, *Vixen* and
many many more masterpieces of local Victorian
atmosphere and unblushing but smiling melodrama
not reprinted?) Lying, looking lazily up at the
stout circle of Cromwell's Castle, I turned back
and opened the Arnold. There, on the printed
page, was the turning-point of my youth, the

moment when in the deserted orchard at Durham I had first, in one swift burning moment, become conscious of the power of poetry.

How miserable I had been that day! Having failed in some school task that morning, been mocked by the form-master and all the class, I had slunk off at lunch-time (it being a half-holiday) and with rage and shame and humiliation in my heart, had hurried home, sat silent and rebellious and glum through luncheon, seen the Arnold in my father's study and, snatching at it, not caring what it was, only wishing to be unnoticed and unspoken-to, had crept away to the orchard. I opened the Matthew Arnold and I read, as once again I read in Tresco:

> They see the Scythian
> On the wide steppe, unharnessing
> His wheel'd house at noon.
> He tethers his beast down, and makes his meal —
> Mares' milk, and bread
> Baked on the embers; — all around
> The boundless, waving grass-plains stretch, thick-
>   starred
> With saffron and the yellow hollyhock
> And flag-leav'd iris-flowers.
> Sitting in his cart

Roman Fountain

He makes his meal: before him, for long miles,
Alive with bright green lizards,
And the springing bustard-fowl,
The track, a straight black line,
Furrows the rich soil: here and there
Clusters of lonely mounds
Topp'd with rough-hewn,
Gray, rain-blear'd statues, overpeer
The sunny waste.

They see the ferry
O'er the broad, clay-laden
Lone Chorasmian stream; — thereon
With snort and strain,
Two horses, strongly swimming, tow
The ferry-boat, with woven ropes
To either bow
Firm-harnessed by the mane; a chief
With shout and shaken spear
Stands at the prow, and guides them; but astern,
The cowering merchants, in long robes,
Sit pale beside their wealth
Of silk-bales and of balsam-drops,
Of gold and ivory,
Of turquoise-earth and amethyst,
Jasper and chalcedony,
And milk-barr'd onyx-stones.
The loaded boat swings groaning
In the yellow eddies;
The Gods behold them.

Roman Fountain

It was the kind of poetry, I suppose, to startle a boy, who was passionate to create but knew not how to choose and select, into a fervour of excitement. It was not so much the poetry, perhaps, as the world that was opened to me, a world of no time, but of detailed and sharp factual beauty.

"I can do this too! I can do this too!" I cried to the gnarled apple-trees, and when old Wallace, the Scotch gardener, as gnarled and as friendly as the apple-trees, appeared down the slope of the garden, I leapt at him and shook him and told him of all that I was going to do.

So now, recalling these two scenes, I looked up from the little shop-windows and thought that round the corners of the street was my Square. I could see from where I stood the rose-umber wall, the church, even a fragment of the tobacconist. I ran forward. Alas, in this little Square there was no Fountain, only an old stone slab with tattered boys sitting on it and kicking their heels.

Almost directly after this a new element was introduced — Frank Gervasi, the representative of the Hearst Press in Rome. I had heard already about Gervasi and, although Michael had told me that he was ' first-class ', ' wonderful ', ' like a brother ', I was a little apprehensive. For he could, if he was a certain kind of man, make things very unpleasant for me.

I saw him on the following Sunday when he, Michael, Hillman and I were to go up to the Alban Hills for lunch and then to the Pope's country home, Castel Gandolfo. The moment I saw him, in the hall of the hotel, I was reassured. I was reassured, in the first place, because of his extraordinary resemblance to Frank Capra. Capra had been a friend in Hollywood. He was one of the few men of genius in the world of the film; he had one of the most beautifully selected and cared-for libraries of first editions I had ever seen; but, far more than either of these, he had a spirit of fire, a merry gaiety and a tender heart. More than these again, he was incalculable. He lived, beyond his work and his love for his family and his friends, a life which I think no one touched. And so, lucky man, Hollywood had never touched him.

Gervasi, I saw at once, had some of that fire and also some of that final reticence. He was of Italian blood but had lived for most of his life in America. He had an American accent and all the American slang, but he was Italian in his warmth of heart, his sudden temper, his physical nearness to the earth, and all that charm that comes from long, long inheritance of the soil — a charm that can belong to no American for many centuries yet. His excitement was intense about anything, about everything. He was reckless, I should fancy, about money and generous to the last penny. He was one of the best journalists in the world; he is also much more than that and there are no bounds to what he may achieve. But I can see him abiding in no place. I see him always with his feet off the ground, fearless, counting no costs, swearing and smiling and crying and singing — his adventures should be an epic.

Meanwhile we sat down in our restaurant on the top of the hill and saw all the Campagna below us like a field of violets struck with silver sparks, while the sun gathered the clouds into his splendour and threw them off again and the shadows moved like thin dark tapestries from corner to corner. This restaurant, like all restaurants to which friends take you, was famous for certain foods and certain wines, and soon we were as merry and noisy as you please.

But it was after Gervasi's arrival that I was aware of the old, old Anglo-American struggle which will, perhaps, never cease so long as this earth lasts. Hillman was the quiet European diplomat

who, indeed, had been in Europe so long that he
knew all the answers to all the questions. But
Gervasi felt everything with such passion that he
could never disguise his opinion — at any rate
when he was with his friends. Not that he and
I had one cross word from first to last, but he
brought out with the intense light of his personality the old American vision of England as a
country whose great history was behind her,
whose word was subtle and double-minded, and,
above all, whose people were patronizing, snob-
bish and supercilious.

On my side, as English as anyone who was
ever born, the things in America that I hated
mingled so hopelessly with the things in America
that I loved that I could never reconcile the
opposites. But this was after Munich and I knew
that many Americans thought that we had deserted Czechoslovakia, while I, on my side, felt
that America had not, since 1919, when she had
so superb an opportunity, done anything at all
to help the world, had been selfish and short-
visioned. I detested her political system, which
seemed to me altogether unworthy of so great
a country, her code of justice, her cheaper
journalism: I loved her vitality, her humour, her
idealism (this last too often blunted by the power

that her less worthy citizens were allowed to exercise). I had lived nearly half of my life in America — some of my dearest friends were, and are, Americans. I did not wish to patronize, but it was as though I were for ever being challenged to defend my country. I did not feel that my country needed defence. With all her faults and mistakes she had, and has, a quality that belongs to no other in the world. The future world — we were all, as we sat in that restaurant, well aware that we were living in the very maelstrom of changing history — needed her and would use her. I do not mean that this Anglo-American undertone of challenge and reply made any difference to the quality of our friendship. It was only that we were, all of us, ever so little on our guard.

After luncheon we motored to Castel Gandolfo. We fell at once into a beautiful jewelled silence. In the restaurant we had been gay and merry and a little drunken. Here, on the square of the town below the Castle and above the Lake, there was a silence that at once quieted us. Gervasi was of course the first to express it. We went into a shop to buy a postcard. Gervasi talked to the woman behind the counter. Afterwards he caught my arm, his eyes burning with his sense of atmosphere, his heart touched by what he felt to be the dramatic pathos of the moment.

"Don't you see, Walpole?" he said. "Don't you feel it? This little place, these poor people, they are lost, bewildered. Down in Rome they are already considering who the next Pope is to be, they have forgotten the last Pope already. But here it is still only of the dead Pope that they are thinking. He isn't yet dead to them. This is the one place in the world perhaps where he is still alive. He was their Father — but literally. He would come up here for his rest, to be cool and quiet. And he would know everyone in the place, their sorrows and sicknesses, when they were in love and when someone died. The whole life of this place depended on his personality. They knew him as no one else knew him — kind, simple, interested in tiny things, warm-hearted and patient.

"The life of this place is suspended. They don't know, of course, who will be the next Pope, but he may be someone who won't care for Castel Gandolfo, who will very seldom come here. All their trade, their colour, their personality may die away. It may become just another little place like thousands of others. But that isn't what they *really* are thinking. They simply are missing a good friend on whom they could rely, who never failed them. They are be-

wildered; you can see it in their faces. They
don't want to talk. They would give all they
have to bring him back to life again."

Certainly it did seem as though the town hung
suspended in the crystal shining air while its fate
was decided.

A path, below the Castle gate, ran to the right
to end in a deserted restaurant with a balcony that hung over the Lake. On the balcony
were the chairs and tables for the customers, looking very desolate, three cats not moving, and a
big empty laundry basket.

Below the terrace, on the side of the hill, were
the green patches of cultivation, every inch used
to advantage, and below the bright green the Lake
of a brilliant turquoise stillness. It seemed to be
made of some fragile tessellated material, itself
also waiting, lifeless but resplendent, until the
word should go forth. On the farther side were
banks of brilliant yellow flowers.

If I dropped a pebble into that Lake what would
happen? There was a stone on the floor of the
terrace and I picked it up. I felt, as I held it in
my hand, that I held the destiny of the world.
Did I lean over the dusty iron balustrade and
drop it down, who knew but the world might
not crack? At least I felt that, with the splash,

the little town would spring to life, trumpets blow, drums be beaten, everyone break into — singing or crying — which would it be?

I held the stone and looked back at the three cats who, unblinking, unmoving, with eyes like filmed marbles, waited for what I would do. No, the time was not yet. It was not thus that, so easily, I might answer that one question that all of us were for ever asking: "What is this for? Where are we going? What is the reason?" I dropped the stone into the laundry basket, and one of the cats, as though the crisis was past, moved and began with steady superior method to wash its leg.

Gervasi said that we would go now into the Castle. He thought that we would be able to see the Astronomer.

Before we went I had one vision of the beauty of this historic place, the road from Frascati to Albano, the fantastic Rocca di Papa, the village like an amphitheatre, high, high up among the pines the tawny ruins of Tusculum, at last the lake of Albano itself. In front of it the ruins of Alba Longa, on the left Monte Cavo, and Castel Gandolfo looking down upon this extinct crater, the turquoise water with its green frame, the pearl-white castle high in the air, where the Papal villa had once been, the villa that Pius XI had so dearly loved. And my mind remained finally resting on the ilex-trees, the ilex-trees, three, four hundred years old, the monstrous ilex-trees with their secrets, their creeping ghosts, their evil wisdom.

All around this place was the history that soon I was to be conscious of so acutely in Rome, the mingling of cruelty and beauty, of sensuousness and asceticism. But not inside these walls. Once I had followed my three friends under that gateway the old Italy was lost and forgotten as though it had never existed.

We stood a little while in the courtyard, surrounded by the plain simple walls, waiting while Gervasi sent his card. Soon there came a message for us — the Astronomer would see us. We climbed stone stairs, came into a room very simply furnished, and there was the Astronomer. He was a short thick-set priest with a voice and face so quiet that you knew he was an astronomer. I have known well four astronomers and they have all had that same quietness and also an under preoccupation. Their manners have always been perfect, but other matters, other horizons, other speculations are in their minds. We ordinary men are separated from astronomers as we are from children, the blind, composers, and, sometimes, poets.

This priest was a Belgian or a Dutchman. He had been the especial friend and companion of the late Pope and he was the last human being I was ever to encounter who grieved passionately for this Pope's going away. When I say ' passionately ' I do not mean that his hair was dishevelled or that he cried or beat his breast. Anything but that. He had a very still smile, the pressure of his hand was warm, he laughed at a joke. But, like the little town below us, he was at a complete loss. For this time even astronomy could not help him.

He took us up into the telescope-room, which interested me because it was an exact small replica of the great one at Mount Wilson where I had been with my friend Hubble and been hit on the nose, all in a second, by Saturn. This was small but very perfect for its purpose, and the Astronomer was so greatly proud of his telescope that he made purring noises like a kettle on the boil. We stood on the roof of the observatory and watched the Campagna crumbling into fragments of sun-dust.

" He was such a very good man," he said about the Pope.

"I know. I am a Protestant, but I was aware of him, read of him, followed what he did, as never with any other Pope."

The Astronomer was delighted. "There! There! I knew it. I always said that the whole world was the better for him. He was so very humble — and very courageous, too."

"Yes, in that last illness . . ."

"When he recovered after they all gave him up! Ah, that was wonderful. He knew that there was still something that had to be done — but it is strange. As it is he went too soon — with the world in the state that it is."

We looked at the visitors' book and all the photographs of the stars. One star-chart is the same to me as another, and if I begin, in the most childish fashion, to consider some of the facts of the spheres — the light-years, the unsighted nebulae — time and distance mean nothing to me, as perhaps they should. My individuality ought also to sink into nothingness. All my worthy friends declare that *they* ' sink into nothingness ' when they consider the stars. Alas, alas, it is not so with me. I rather feel how great and wonderful is Man that he can discover these wonders — and I am a man with other men.

"Did the Pope," I asked tentatively, " ever feel

depressed when he looked through the telescope at the utter insignificance of man?"

The Astronomer smiled his still smile. "The Pope considered each end of the scale of a wonderful grandeur — the farthest star known to man and the new-born child at its mother's breast. Miracles on every side. Only God can explain them."

"His tastes and habits were very simple?"

"Very. He liked fruit and cheese and eggs. He worked so very hard. He had great physical strength. Everyone loved him."

His voice caught. I am sure that he was a most unsentimental man, but I realized at that moment that his own loss was irrecoverable. I had often turned over in my mind how it would be for me if I lost through death the human being I loved most deeply. I did not consider it sentimentally but as a practical fact. I had lived long enough to realize that when a friend dies your life is not over, you are not wretched for ever more, but your life is *changed*. There will never again be anyone like *that* person. In their life you tolerated, you were careless, critical, lazy, selfish. Only after physical death do you grasp that *uniqueness* — my father, my mother, Hubert Henry Davies, Henry James, Ethel McKenna, Conrad, Tom Herbert, Boley —

how strangely they are illuminated now, these figures, by their uniqueness. How I love them because, in life, I did them the wrong of taking them so often for granted.

So now the Astronomer looked at me, his hand fumbling his black sleeves, his eyes clouded. I knew, too, that I was saying an absolute farewell now to this Pope who had been so much in my mind. Here in this very simple room that had the smell of apples, of cheese and of irises. I liked the Astronomer so very much and the kindliness and sweetness of this house that I had a moment's disgust at the thought of returning to Rome.

But this was the closing of half my adventure, and already, as we left the Castle and turned into the Square, the second half was beginning.

XIV

AND now came a fortnight when I was entirely alone with myself and Rome. I don't mean by that that I had not to write my daily article (although Hillman let me off some of these), that I did not see Noyes and the others constantly — but I had no real contact, during this time, with any of them. The contact was to return.

Meanwhile it was as though my guardian saint — a mixture, I think, of St. Porphyrio and Boleslavski, my Polish friend in Hollywood. Do you know about St. Porphyrio who collected tortoises and grew an especial kind of rose in the desert? There is a lot about him in Jean Paul. Boley, who was a giant in body and in heart, was ideally constructed for anyone's patron saint —

patient, broad-shouldered, the very man for crossing streams, and so real to me now as I write that I can feel his hand on my shoulder. Anyway, it was as though my guardian saint whispered in my ear: " You are to be alone for a bit so that you may see one or two things uninterrupted."

It was during this fortnight that I touched ever so lightly the dark stained stones of old Rome, that I found my restaurant, that I bought ten bronzes, that I thought I saw Michael Angelo one evening at the cinema — so that I did not really miss my time!

First as to the restaurant. I won't give it its real name; I will call it the ' Vittorio '. In any case it was one day between the hours of one and two and nearer two than one — the beginning of the siesta, in fact, when there is no life in the town and no self-respecting person wishes to be served. But I had been working late in the hotel at this very book — and I picked up my hat and rushed out of the hotel and down the Spanish Steps and past the book-shop where, when I asked for Zola's *Rome*, the young man thought I meant a guide-book — down the little street with the antiques, the chocolate cakes and the silver fish-knives, into the Corso, and there — whether to left or right I shall not say — was the restaurant.

Roman Fountain

I entered it and there was no one there at all. I could have stolen anything I liked except that there was nothing to steal save a tortoiseshell cat, some tables and three large glass mirrors. Oh yes, and a portrait of Mussolini. After a while a waiter appeared, rubbing his eyes, and I partook of the best vegetable soup and the richest *gnocchi* I had yet enjoyed in Rome. I was just finishing these when a man of about sixty, rather white-faced and weary, appeared and asked me whether I would like some chocolate cake. I said I would. The chocolate cake appeared. Oh Heaven! Oh Paradise! No chocolate cake anywhere is like this chocolate cake nor ever will be again. It does not at all resemble that sodden composition in England, a damp sponge with layers of soggy chocolate. No, in this the chocolate rises in tight, sharp little curls on the top. The cake itself is brittle so that the very crumbs have life of their own and every fragment is taut and crystal. The sweetness is not cloying but rather wooing and lustful as though it would say: " Come closer! Come closer! The climax is yet to arrive! "

Such is the sweetness, in fact, that my dear sister, who is a doctor, would die of horror did she see me eating this cake. For I am not supposed to eat sweet things and will die the sooner if I do.

Roman Fountain

In this matter did I first meet Paolo, who was more important than the chocolate cake. Paolo, like so many Italian waiters, had lived and worked in London for many years and had even played football for Chelsea. He loved England although he detested its climate, its cabbage, its Sundays and its Anthony Eden. During all the time I was with him Mr. Eden was the only subject on this earth that made his pale cheeks red, and, when I enquired the reason, his feeling became so personal that I was very glad indeed that Mr. Eden was not present — hating all rows unless I happen to be very angry myself.

Paolo, I came to believe, was the ideal Italian. Intensely patriotic but not narrowly provincial, devoted to his wife and children (he had a son just off to college), perfect at his job, and, best of all, through his melancholy eyes there gleamed always that cynical, unrestrainable Italian jest, irony, irony, irony, so that all things — even Mussolini and the lusts of the flesh — are clothed, at the last and most ultimate, ironically.

So much for the ' Vittorio ' and Paolo. They were both to become of great importance to me.

Very seriously I discovered that the past was creeping in upon the present. It was as though the discovery — or rather the moment of discovery — when it arrived would be complete like a gleaming, glittering crystal ball, or, possibly, Henry James' golden bowl, but without any flaw to it. To attain this completeness one element after another in its nature must be presented to me. Even Mr. Garside might, I was beginning to think, be an element. Certainly the visits to Keats' grave, the memory of Mr. Montmorency, my mother, the Durham orchard, the first days in London, the Cumberland garden, all these played their part.

And now Pope Julius, Niccolò de' Niccoli, Girolamo Olgiati, Aldo Manuzio and many many more began to creep into my consciousness. This is not a work of erudition. I am not a historian and most certainly not a philosopher, but these men, through Symonds, through stories told to me, through pieces of Ranke, through bits of this and pieces of that, approached as they would and must a novelist — that is romantically, as figures standing for something behind them and more important than they.

Pope Julius II was, of course, Michael Angelo's Pope. With the help of Bramante he designed St. Peter's, and he tortured Michael Angelo. He was never happy unless fighting and, to quote

Symonds, ' he drowned the peninsula in blood '. He was both the saviour of the country and the curse of Italy. A thin, bent, horrible grand old man with fire in his eyes.

Niccolò de' Niccoli was quite another. He was a copyist and collector, but also very much more than that. Just consider the joy he must have felt when one day he received a manuscript containing seven tragedies of Sophocles, six of Aeschylus, and the *Argonautica* of Apollonius Rhodius. But, as I say, he was very much more than a collector although Florence owed him a vast debt in this alone. He was considered the final judge of his time on literary style, and any scholar of repute would submit his manuscript to him before daring to print it. He was not, however, himself an author.

I like so much this description of his personal life that I must quote it:

First of all, he was of a most fair presence; lively, for a smile was ever on his lips; and very pleasant in his talk. He wore clothes of the fairest crimson cloth, down to the ground. He never married in order that he might not be impeded in his studies. He was above all men the most cleanly in eating, as also in all other things. When he sat at table, he ate from fair antique vases; and, in like manner, all his table was covered

with porcelain and other vessels of great beauty.
The cup from which he drank was of crystal or of
some other precious stone. To see him at table—
a perfect model of the men of old—was of truth a
charming sight. He always willed that all the napkins
set before him should be of the whitest, as well as
all the linen. Some might wonder at the many
vases he possessed, to whom I answer that things of
that sort were neither so highly valued then, nor so
much regarded, as they have since become; and
Niccolò having friends everywhere, anyone who
wished to do him a pleasure would send him marble
statues, or antique vases, carvings, inscriptions,
pictures from the hands of distinguished masters, and
mosaic tablets. He had a most beautiful map, on
which all the parts and cities of the world were
marked; others of Italy and Spain, all painted.
Florence could not show a house more full of ornaments than his, or one that had in it a greater number
of graceful objects, so that all who went there found
innumerable things of worth to please varieties of taste.

Is not that beautiful, with the crimson gown,
the snow-white napkins, the crystal goblet, the
splendid map of brilliant colours ' with all the
parts and cities of the world '? It is like a clear,
sharp jewelled portrait by Quentin Matsys.

Girolamo Olgiati again was another story. He
was one of the three young nobles of Milan who

struck down the despot, Galeazzo Sforza. Sforza had outraged Olgiati's sister. First they received the sacrament in St. Stephen's Church, then:

On the morning of December 26, 1476, the duke entered San Stefano. At one and the same moment the daggers of the three conspirators struck him — Olgiati's in the breast, Visconti's in the back, Lampagnani's in the belly. He cried " Ah, Dio ! " and fell dead upon the pavement. The friends were unable to make their escape: Visconti and Lampagnani were killed on the spot. Olgiati was seized, tortured and torn to death.

It is in his torture that he comes to me so clearly. He was very handsome: he was only twenty-two. Throughout the horrible torture he carried himself with a marvellous gaiety. To the priest asking him to repent he replied: " As for the noble action for which I am about to die, it is this that gives me peace; to this I trust for pardon from the Judge of all. Far from repenting, if I had to come ten times to life in order ten times to die by these same torments, I should not hesitate to dedicate my blood and all my powers to an object so sublime." When the hangman stood above him, ready to begin the work of mutilation, he is said to have exclaimed, " Mors acerba, fama perpetua, stabit vetus memoria facti " (" My death is untimely, my fame eternal, the memory of the deed will last for aye ").

Aldo Manuzio is of course quite another figure. He was born (his name in reality Teobaldo Mannucci) in 1450 at Sermoneta, near Velletri. He always signed his publications with his full titles — Aldus Pius Manutius Romanus et Philhellen. He studied Latin at Rome. It was Prince Alberto Pio, master of the little town of Carpi, who helped Aldo with the necessary funds for starting his printing press. So the history of the whole world is changed, and the little town of Carpi, so Symonds says, was not, in his time, even mentioned in Murray's *Handbook*!

Aldo's idea was to print the whole literature of Greece! In Carpi he established a Greek Press. It is no intention of mine to tell his life story, but through every possible difficulty and interruption, while the French deluged Brescia with blood, and Venice was temporarily ruined by the forces of the League of Cambray, Aldo never ceased, never flagged. When I think of the nonsense I've heard during the last year or two from whimpering cowards about the end of civilization! They should read a little of the history of Mediaeval Italy if they want to know what civilization can endure and survive! Aldo formed a company but in the end died poor. Erasmus accused him of avarice. Men are always accused of avarice when they are straining body and soul for the creation of some great work.

Erasmus visited Aldo in 1508, and there is a pleasant picture of the two great men together. He personally superintended the re-impression of his *Proverbs*. Erasmus says: ' Together we attacked the work, I writing, while Aldo gave my copy to the Press '. Symonds adds: ' In one corner of the room sat the scholar at his desk with the thin keen face so well portrayed by Holbein, improvising new paragraphs, and making additions to his previous collections in the brilliant Latin style that no one else could write '.

So here they are, these very different men — Niccolò de' Niccoli, Girolamo Olgiati, Pope Julius, Aldo Manuzio. There are of course hundreds and hundreds more. I have purposely said nothing about the most famous — Cellini, Machiavelli, Petrarch, Savonarola, Boccaccio. . . . But these few — the bloodthirsty Pope, the young hero, the scholar, the printer — how eager and vital and exciting a world they instantly make of themselves! How savage a world also! But what vitality!

Roman Fountain

And at once when one has only touched the
very surface of this violent, barbaric, cultured
civilization there appears that same old eternal
question, the question that now in Rome everything was driving me to ask. I have placed it as
a motto to my book in the casual impertinent
words of Wystan Auden:

> It's no use raising a shout,
> No, Honey, you can cut that right out.
> I don't want any more hugs;
> Make me some fresh tea, fetch me some rugs.
> Here am I, here are you:
> But what does it mean? What are we going to do?
>
> Here am I, here are you:
> But what does it mean? What are we going to do?

I am an artist. Of this sort or that sort, what
does it matter? The making of things of beauty,
irrespective of gain, of glory, of rewards, seems
to me the finest job for a human being to concern
himself with — the one job that is selfless and
may be enduring. I include the priest and the
physician in this company.

Well, nothing notable was produced in Italy
between the thirteenth and the seventeenth centuries that did not bear the stamp and character

of fine art, and thousands upon thousands of men with Niccolò and Pius and Aldo were concerned, with all their energies, all their resources, body and soul, in this project. Why did they do it? What drove them? What were they after?

> Here am I, here are you:
> But what does it mean? What are we going to do?

Painting is the art in which the Italians among all the nations of the modern world stand unapproachable. What were the Italian painters trying to do? Here, it seems to me, you raise at once the deep abiding question that this Papal business was raising for me now in Rome. In what world do you, artist and creator, or simply man who is having his experience of this life, believe?

It was the business of the Italian painters to give form to the ideas evolved by Christianity, but so soon as they begin to do this the two worlds come into sharp conflict. The human intellect was newly freed, but Christian and Pagan traditions were now in close contact and struggling with one another for mastery. The Greeks thought of their gods as incarnate persons and all the artist had to see to was that this incarnate personality should be impressive. Christianity, on the other hand, made the moral and spiritual nature of man all-essential. The body and the things of the body had a subordinate place in the system. But, for the artist, beauty comes first, morality second. For the Christian, morality is altogether first. And today when dogmas matter very little, the struggle is as acute as ever. Without a belief in some kind of spiritual world the artist is only half an artist — his love of beauty becomes of itself a spiritual belief. But what of morality, of goodness, of truth and self-sacrifice, of love for the world and the people in it? Has the artist any concern in these things? Is he the less of an artist if he has?

As I peered myopically back I saw the two worlds, spiritual and physical, most violently contrasted. The cruelty, savagery, lust and greed of this old world is like a rich, restless madness. But Christianity is in its roots ascetic. Symonds says of himself: "I cannot read the New Testament, the *Imitatio Christi*, the *Confessions of St. Augustine* and the *Pilgrim's Progress* without feeling that Christianity in its origin, and as understood by its chief champions, was and is ascetic".

And yet does not the religion of Jesus Christ spread much further and involve much more?

Roman Fountain

Would not Christ, with much gladness, have sat
down beside Niccolò in his crimson gown and
drunk out of the crystal goblets, and would He
not happily have watched Erasmus and Aldo at
the *Proverbs*?

We may realize how acute the conflict soon
became when we read the story of Fra Bartolom-
meo, the disciple of Savonarola, who painted a
St. Sebastian in the cloister of San Marco. Soon
the Dominican priests were aware through the
confessions of their female penitents that this
picture was a snarer of souls The picture
disappeared. No one, so far as is known, ever
saw it again. All the virtues were represented in
it — fortitude, spiritual constancy, ecstasy — but
the naked body of the young man was extremely
handsome. The strange fact was, as Symonds says,
that painting, "notwithstanding the range and
wealth of its resources, could not deal with the
motives of Christianity so successfully as sculpture
with the myths of Paganism. . . . Art is essen-
tially and uncontrollably free, and what is more,
is free precisely in that realm of sensuous delight-
fulness from which cloistral religion turns aside to
seek her own ecstatic liberty of contemplation."
With the sensuality went the cruelty.

Roman Fountain

I will spend no time here over the horrible sadistic tortures of the mediaeval world. Example after example can be found only too easily. There was, for instance, Galeazzo Sforza whom Olgiati slew. He would feed his victims elaborately on unspeakable abominations, bury them alive, spend days in devising new and intricate tortures. Or there is Caesar Borgia, a very complicated and in some ways noble character, who, to give his father, Alexander, pleasure and to amuse himself, turned out some prisoners sentenced to death in a court-yard of the palace, arrayed himself in fantastic clothes and amused the Papal party by shooting the unlucky criminals. They ran round and round the court crouching and doubling to avoid his arrows, he, to encourage them, calling out that the one who survived to the last should be spared. The Pope and Lucrezia looked on with applauding laughter.

All this and much more can be found in the pages of Symonds and the historians.

It is these elements of lust and creative beauty and mysticism coming together so that they make a figure of splendour and horror and supplication that arose out of the stones of old Rome to mingle for me with the present.

When the mist cleared and the words were

read and the books closed it was Michael Angelo Buonarroti who stood beside me. He had been always clearer to me, I think, than any other figure of the Renaissance, except Cervantes. I had read some little book about him when I was a child and I never lost him after that.

Here is Condivi's description of him:

Michaelangelo is of good complexion; more muscular and bony than fat or fleshy in his person: healthy above all things, as well by reason of his natural constitution as of the exercise he takes, and habitual continence in food and sexual indulgence. Nevertheless he was a weakly child, and has suffered two illnesses in manhood. His countenance always shows a good and wholesome colour. Of stature he is as follows: height middling; broad in the shoulders; the rest of the body somewhat slender in proportion. The shape of his face is oval, the space above the ears being one-sixth higher than a semicircle. Consequently the temples project beyond the ears, and the ears beyond the cheeks, and these beyond the rest; so that the skull, in relation to the whole head, must be called large. The forehead, seen in front, is square; the nose, a little flattened — not by nature, but because, when he was a young boy, Torrigiano di Torrigiani, a brutal and insolent fellow, smashed in the cartilage with his fist. Michaelangelo was carried home half-dead on this occasion, and

Torrigiano, having been exiled from Florence for his violence, came to a bad end. The nose, however, being what it is, bears a proper proportion to the forehead and the rest of the face. The lips are thin, but the lower is slightly thicker than the upper; so that, seen in profile, it projects a little. The chin is well in harmony with the features I have described. The forehead, in a side view, almost hangs over the nose; and this looks hardly less than broken, were it not for a trifling protuberance in the middle. The eyebrows are not thick with hair; the eyes may even be called small, of a colour like horn, but speckled and stained with spots of bluish yellow. The ears in good proportion; hair of the head black, as also the beard, except that both are now grizzled by old age; the beard double-forked, about five inches long, and not very bushy, as may partly be observed in his portrait.

Is not this a splendid portrait of a man? Buonarroti is here for ever, alive, speaking, moving, breathing as no other artist in the world for me save Walter Scott and Keats — and these three are, with Cézanne, the men I love most dearly in the whole eternal world of art.

Can you not see him standing there? Muscular and bony, of a healthy colour, middling height, broad in the shoulders, his body tapering away — the large head, the overhanging forehead, the

broken nose, the beard and, above all, the eyes
' small, of a colour like horn ' with the brown
lights — yes, and the pouting lower lip. A man
who, like Cézanne, had to fight the whole of his
time. He fought everybody and everything, his
patrons, his art, and himself.

I do not doubt that his nature was homosexual,
as was Leonardo's and El Greco's; he was only
the worse for that in that he was a lonely man.
All men are lonely, but those with a twisted
sexual nature are loneliest of all; which does not
mean that they are not happy. Only, in their
experience, they are by themselves. This is what
I feel of Michael Angelo: that he was always by
himself. That does not mean that he did not
love anybody. He loved his parents and helped
his brothers. They were none of them worthy
of him.

Here is one of his letters to his father:

Dearest Father,
Your last informs me how things are going on
at Florence, although I already knew something. We
must have patience, commit ourselves to God, and
repent of our sins; for these trials are solely due to
them, and more particularly to pride and ingratitude.
I never conversed with a people more ungrateful and
puffed up than the Florentines. Therefore, if judge-

ment comes, it is but right and reasonable. As for the sixty ducats you tell me you are fined, I think this a scurvy trick, and am exceedingly annoyed. However, we must have patience as long as it pleases God. I will write and enclose two lines to Giuliano de' Medici. Read them, and if you like to present them to him, do so; you will see whether they are likely to be of any use. If not, consider whether we can sell our property and go to live elsewhere. . . . Look to your life and health; and if you cannot share the honours of the land like other burghers, be contented that bread does not fail you, and live well with Christ, and poorly, as I do here; for I live in a sordid way, regarding neither life nor honours — that is, the world — and suffer the greatest hardships and innumerable anxieties and dreads. It is now about fifteen years since I had a single hour of well-being, and all that I have done has been to help you, and you have never recognized this nor believed it. God pardon us all! I am ready to go on doing the same so long as I live, if only I am able.

Much of this letter, word for word, might have been written by Cézanne. Like Cézanne he was for ever growling and grumbling; they had both of them one of the greatest gifts God can give a man — absolute single-mindedness of purpose.

And here is a poem of his to Giovanni da Pistoja to show what he thought of himself:

Roman Fountain

I've grown a goitre by dwelling in this den —
As cats from stagnant streams in Lombardy,
Or in what other land they hap to be —
Which drives the belly close beneath the chin:
My beard turns up to heaven; my nape falls in
Fixed on my spine; my breastbone visibly
Grows like a harp; a rich embroidery
Bedews my face from brush-drops thick and thin,
My loins into my paunch like levers grind;
My buttock like a crupper bears my weight;
My feet unguided wander to and fro;
In front my skin grows loose and long; behind,
By bending it becomes more taut and strait;
Crosswise I strain me like a Syrian bow:
Whence false and quaint, I know,
Must be the fruit of squinting brain and eye;
For ill can aim the gun that bends awry.
Come then, Giovanni, try
To succour my dead pictures and my fame,
Since foul I fare and painting is my shame.

How greatly he must have enjoyed writing that!

As to his works I will say very little because everyone else has said so much. You must, of course, combine Florence and Rome and think of them, in his case, together. But here I was in Rome and especially, from now onwards, in and around the Sistine Chapel. First, as a young and ardent tourist, I had lain on my back and looked on the ceiling through a glass. Now it was to be as though those paintings had become my own.

Michael Angelo's fate rests in these words of Condivi's:

Having reached Rome, many months elapsed before Julius decided on what great work he would employ him (Michael Angelo). At last it occurred to him to use his genius in the construction of his own tomb. The design furnished by Michel Angelo pleased the Pope so much that he sent him off immediately to Carrara, with commission to quarry as much marble as was needful for that undertaking. Two thousand ducats were put to his credit with Alamanni Salviati at Florence for expenses. He remained more than eight months among those mountains, with two servants and a horse, but without any salary except his keep. One day, while inspecting the locality, the fancy took him to convert a hill which commands the seashore into a Colossus, visible by mariners afar. The shape of the huge rock, which lent itself admirably to such a purpose, attracted him, and he was further moved to emulate the ancients, who, sojourning in the place peradventure with the same object as himself, in order to while away the time, or for some other motive, have left certain unfinished and rough-hewn monuments, which gave a good specimen of their craft. And assuredly he would have carried out this scheme if time enough had been at his disposal, or if the special purpose of his visit to Carrara had permitted. I one day heard him lament bitterly that he had not done so.

The whole of Michael Angelo's life and art lies revealed in these sentences — the Pope's meanness and grand egoism, the artist's genius, inspired visions, hardship of life, ceaseless vitality, divine ambition, independence of mind. The most revealing phrase of all is: "if the special purpose of his visit to Carrara had permitted". For he had to live, to depend on the will and caprice of his arrogant and tyrannical patrons, to fight his jealous enemies, and to turn aside, again and again, from the darling visions of his heart.

That Tomb of the Pope he carried on his back for the rest of his days, and even after he was dead, his enemies, to spite him, spoiled his superb vision of St. Peter's. However, it is as part of my Roman adventure that I think of him, and in Rome is the Sistine Chapel.

The miracle of the vault of the Sistine Chapel to myself is the sublimation of the nervous energy of the individual figures into the calm and lovely spirit of the whole. Michael Angelo is principally criticized, I suppose, because of this same nervous energy and exaggeration of limb and movement. Symonds is poetically eloquent on this:

Roman Fountain

The violence of Michelangelo, unlike that of Luca, lay not so much in the choice of savage subjects (cruelty, ferocity, extreme physical and mental torment) as in a forceful, passionate, tempestuous way of handling all the themes he treated.

The angels of the Judgment, sustaining the symbols of Christ's Passion, wrestle and bend their agitated limbs like athletes. Christ emerges from the sepulchre, not in victorious tranquillity, but with the clash and clangour of an irresistible energy set free. Even in the Crucifixion, one leg has been wrenched away from the nail which pierced its foot, and writhes round the knee of the other still left riven to the cross.

The loves of Leda and the Swan, of Ixion and Juno, are spasms of voluptuous pain; the sleep of the Night is troubled with fantastic dreams, and the Dawn starts into consciousness with a shudder of prophetic anguish. There is not a hand, a torso, a simple nude, sketched by this extraordinary master, which does not vibrate with nervous tension, as though the fingers that grasped the pen were clenched and the eyes that viewed the model glowed beneath knit brows. Michelangelo, in fact, saw nothing, felt nothing, interpreted nothing, on exactly the same lines as anyone who had preceded or who followed him. His imperious personality he stamped upon the smallest trifle of his work.

That is well said. How marvellous are the

photographs of the drawings that I bought at the Michael Angelo House in Florence! There is something deeply moving and astonishing in the consideration of this little man with the broken nose and the eyes of horn releasing into the world for ever and ever this force of vital, moving, striving, fighting beauty! And yet, after a time, when one has drunk it all in and absorbed it, when one has sat, as I did often during these next days, in one of the Cardinals' stalls in the Sistine Chapel, gazing upwards and not moving, one seems to reach, after the turbulence and striving, a world of deep calm and omnipotent tranquillity.

Adam, lying on his side, looking so humbly, so trustfully at God the Father, is not turbulent. The wonderful Christ in the unfinished painting in the National Gallery is not turbulent, the Pietà in St. Peter's is not turbulent, and I am not sure that " the sleep of the Night is troubled with fantastic dreams ".

It seems to me that with all the distress and frustration and agonies of his own life Michael Angelo was not unaware of the other world behind the unsatisfactory noisy one of cheating, penurious Pope, plotting rivals, disappointing relatives. And at the last I see him, after all his disappointments and grumblings, his sordid living

and tireless working, his unapproachable alone-
ness, as, apart from his genius, a simple loving
man who cared passionately for those dear to him.

One more letter to his father and I have done:

DEAREST FATHER,

I marvelled much at what had happened to you
the other day, when I did not find you at home. And
now, hearing that you complain of me, and say that
I have turned you out of doors, I marvel much the
more, inasmuch as I know for certain that never once
from the day that I was born till now had I a single
thought of doing anything or small or great which
went against you; and all this time the labours I have
undergone have been for love of you alone. Since I
returned from Rome to Florence, you know that I
have always cared for you, and you know that all that
belongs to me I have bestowed on you. Some days
ago, then, when you were ill, I promised solemnly
never to fail you in anything within the scope of my
whole faculties so long as my life lasts; and this I again
affirm. Now I am amazed that you should have forgotten everything so soon. And yet you have learned
to know me by experience these thirty years, you
and your sons, and are well aware that I have always
thought and acted, so far as I was able, for your good.

How can you go about saying I have turned you
out of doors? Do you not see what a reputation you
have given me by saying I turned you out? Only this
was wanting to complete my tale of troubles, all of

which I suffer for your love. You repay me well, forsooth. But let it be as it must: I am willing to acknowledge that I have always brought shame and loss on you, and on this supposition I beg your pardon. Reckon that you are pardoning a son who has lived a bad life, and done you all the harm which it is possible to do. And so I once again implore you to pardon me, scoundrel that I am, and not bring on me the reproach of having turned you out of doors; for that matters more than you imagine to me. After all, I am your son.

' That matters more than you imagine to me. After all, I am your son.'

After reading that letter I shall not be afraid of Michael Angelo when I meet him.

XV

MR. GARSIDE, stopping me in the hall of the Ambassadors, said, " Oh, by the way, there's something I want to ask your advice on."

I was in a great hurry and was carrying a pot of camellias which I had bought down the street and insisted on carrying home myself because I was afraid that it might not be the same pot of camellias if I didn't.

But Mr. Garside had a way with him, and this way was to conceive it quite impossible that anybody should do other than he wished him to do. He was neither bully nor tyrant but simply lacking in all sensitive imagination. We passed into the bare and unsympathetic saloon, I carrying my pot of flowers before me as Mary Queen of Scots carried her ivory crucifix when walking to the block. I placed the flowers on a table and smiled with pleasure as I perceived a new fat waxen Victorian bud. Mr. Garside had not even noticed that I was carrying a flower-pot because he was intent on what he was going to say. He had a one-track mind.

If he had noticed he would have been shocked and suspected my morals, and that would have both horrified and intrigued him. However, as it was, he stood above me in his immaculate but inhuman clothing and seriously addressed me. He was wearing a white slip to his waistcoat, and dove-coloured spats — both so old-fashioned that he looked like a rather elderly hero of a Daly comedy.

" I've heard," he said, " that you are well known for helping younger writers."

He paused and beamed at me as though I would be highly delighted at this. But I had heard it before: it had even been said that when I helped a younger writer no one ever bought any of his books again. Altogether I counted as a fool, always, anyone who paid me that particular compliment. But Mr. Garside, being sure in his own mind that he had especially pleased me, was so greatly pleased with *himself* that I was a dim scarcely-visioned figure in his glazing eye.

" The fact is there's a young fellow in the office at home that wants to write. In fact he *has* written — several things."

" What? " I asked, looking at my camellias.

" A skit for our operatic society — damned clever. He didn't do it all, but here and there, you know. He tells me he's sent several things to the papers, too — one about Freedom, I think he said, and another about Motoring in Wales. The point is my wife tells me he's written a novel — in her last letter. I've got it upstairs."

" What's the novel about? "

" She doesn't say. It's sure to be clever. But a man like you must know all the ropes. My wife tells me she's read all your novels, simply the whole lot. My wife's your fan. She is really. While I was in my bath this morning it suddenly occurred to me that you'd be the very man. If you'd read the boy's book it would be a tremendous help to him, and then give him some advice — point out where the thing's wrong, read over some bits with him. He's a nice boy, I know he'll take it all right."

I stared at Mr. Garside fascinated. " No writer can help another writer," I enunciated. And I thought of the past. Of all those who had been so good to me — Henry James, Wells, Bennett,

Galsworthy, and, especially perhaps, in the old days in Charles Street, Somerset Maugham with his hospitality, his generosity, his practical common sense. And not a one of them had been of the slightest use to my writing. Of my books only *Mr. Perrin*, *The Dark Forest*, *The Old Ladies* had appealed to other writers. I was not a writer's writer, having no new technical tricks to offer and being, in any case, an 'unoriginal'. But I had this sop at least to feed my pride with. I had been altogether unable to pick up anything from anybody.

So I said to Mr. Garside: "It's no use, Mr. Garside. I never read manuscripts any more. What the young writer wants is praise: even if he doesn't know it, that's what he wants. If you don't praise him he thinks you a fool. If you do praise him he thinks he's great — not because you've *praised* him but because you've confirmed his own secret ideas about himself."

" Oh, you're quite wrong about this young chap."

" No, I'm not. We're all the same. Besides there's another thing — I've only got a limited amount of time."

Mr. Garside looked incredulous.

" Yes, really. I have to earn my living, I have a lot of letters to answer, I have to read books for review: even, at times, I have to *think*."

Mr. Garside grinned rather as a man grins when another has whispered him a bawdy story in the presence of ladies.

" Oh, I know all that about work."

" It's true, I assure you. But the main thing is that one writer cannot help another writer. Really that's true. If you're an artist making something there are only two things that matter — have you made what you intended to make, and are you an artist whose personality is interesting enough to justify your making anything?"

But Mr. Garside hadn't listened to this. He wasn't interested in artists. I could see that he was disappointed in me. I knew that back in England he would say: "I met Hugh Walpole, the novelist, in Rome. He was all right. A bit selfish. What I mean is that he thinks of himself first — won't put himself out, if you know what I mean."

However, there it was, and as a man of the world changes the conversation from a dangerous topic to a safe one, Mr. Garside asked me lightly who, in my opinion, the next Pope would be. For that was where we now were.

I was at length nearing the very centre; from now onwards my work would be inside the Vatican.

Roman Fountain

I went with Michael to watch them preparing to build-in the rooms and corridors where the Cardinals would be confined during the Conclave. I felt at once that I was living now in a world that I should never understand and to which I should never belong. But from its mystery I might carry an experience which would enrich my own development. What I could not understand was the surrender of Reason: in this I was right, for, some months later, I was to see the face of a friend that had been tender, kind, sympathetic, quite suddenly, at the mention of Joyce's *Ulysses*, furious, cruel, evil — incomprehensible altogether to my own tolerance. And also to my weakness. For I realized that in this resolution towards fanatical obedience, there was a fine self-sacrificing faith. Only the intelligence, it seemed to me, had to submit to blindfolding — yes, but only perhaps that it might see the more clearly.

In any case, as I walked with Michael through the Hall of the Pontiffs, I listened to some facts. No one knows by whom the first Vatican Palace was built. Charlemagne was here and Leo III crowned him in St. Peter's in 800. It was the return of Gregory XI from Avignon that marked the beginning of the use of the Vatican by the Popes. The first Conclave was held in 1380.

Nicholas V, the first Renaissance Pope, was the first to embellish the Vatican. ' Embellish ' is a good word and some of the embellishment is good and some of it not so good. So much for history. Nobody cares. Or only a very few.

The two things I like, if you call them embellishments, are the Loggia of Raphael and the Chapel of Fra Angelico. Raphael is, as a rule, not meant for me, nor am I meant for Raphael. What I mean is sufficiently shocking — namely that I would rather have a scribbled tree-trunk by Titian than a whole Madonna by Raphael. But here in this glowing sunny passage there is nothing but loveliness — flowers, leaves, and so many little animals all perpetually happy in perpetual sunshine. There is a small bird with wings of gold and a half-open eye. All ecstatic recognition of the excellence of life is in that small staring eye. And, by Fra Angelico, I love the Ordination of St. Laurence. But this book is in no way a guide to the pictures of Rome. There are so many books that do that so well.

I stood in a courtyard with Michael and looked upward to see them boarding up the windows of the rooms where the Cardinals would sleep during the Conclave. We ascended in a lift and walked precariously on boards and looked through doors into the spare, empty little rooms where the Cardinals would sleep. Each Cardinal would be attended by his secretary. Each Cardinal would have a separate bath. A workman, thick-set, with dark hair and sparkling black eyes, looked at me as though he knew me, and just as I passed him said:

" Mister — how about Piccadilly? "

" It's all right," I said.

He sat up resting back on his thick haunches, his round brown head thrown back like a bird's.

" Where did you learn your English? "

He dropped his voice. I stood close to him and there was no one near to us.

" Curzon Street."

" Curzon Street? " I was extremely astonished.

" Yes. I want to go back. Take me, sir."

" But what should I do with you? " I was amused.

"I clean your shoes, wash your shirts, cook spaghetti."

" Are you married? "

" Yes — and four children."

" What will you do with them? "

" Ah, they stay here. They have a good mother."

" But you will miss them."

Roman Fountain

" They come later."

" Give me your address. Perhaps I will write to you."

He scribbled it on a piece of paper from his pocket. His eyes followed me, dancing, lively like water in sunshine, trying to escape.

It was perhaps from him that I got this sense of claustrophobia. They were enclosing something in the Vatican. Pius XI had escaped. Even now he was circling, on steady white wings, a bird with shining black eyes, above the observatory at Castel Gandolfo. Now they were making preparations to catch and imprison someone else. It was extraordinary the impression that I had, as I followed Michael, of Pius XI, free, happy, flying, flying above Raphael's leaves and flowers. No one any more could catch him.

So the little workman, with the sparkling eyes, wanted to escape. And Mussolini, perhaps, also. When I went home that afternoon I found Severn's letter about Keats as he lay dying in that stifling room on the side of the Steps:

Tortonia, the banker, has refused us any more money; the bill is returned unaccepted, and to-morrow I must pay my last crown for this accursed lodging-place; and, what is more, if he dies, all the beds and furniture will be burnt and the walls scraped, and they will come on me for a hundred pounds or more! But, above all, this noble fellow lying on the bed and without the common spiritual comforts that many a rogue and fool has in his last moments! . . .

If I could leave Keats every day for a time I could soon raise money by my painting, but he will not let me out of his sight, he will not bear the face of a stranger. I would rather cut my tongue out than tell him I must get the money — that would kill him at a word. You see my hopes of being kept by the Royal Academy will be cut off unless I send a picture by the spring. . . . Keats sees all this — his knowledge of anatomy makes every change tenfold worse; every way he is unfortunate, yet everyone offers me assistance on his account. He cannot read any letters, he has made me put them by him unopened. They tear him to pieces — he dare not look on the outside of any more: make this known.

The prisoners! The prisoners! I felt as though the whole of Rome were a prison that night.

Then came the day when the Cardinals were to pass, in the face of the world, into their seclusion. But before this we were taken into the Sistine Chapel to see how it looked at this last moment before the Conclave. How very different from that first vision I had had of it when, as a boy, I had leaned back, looked through the little glass at Michael Angelo's Adam, felt that I was in the very stronghold of God the Father.

Now the room was filled with journalists. The Cardinals' chairs were ranged against the painted walls, in their velvet, with their canopies, a little table in front of each. We were photographed sitting in them. "If you don't mind — a little to the right. Now. Leaning forward — that's it exactly." In this very chair a Cardinal would sit and record his vote: perhaps the future Pope.

"Now, Gervasi, stand talking to him. About anything. Look up a minute."

But the great difference between that first visit and this present one was that now I was closer to Michael Angelo himself. Not only was I aware of the grumbling, shabby, brave old man but I felt that he was himself conscious of me. What egotism! And yet not so, for he must understand now the universality of love and that we are all held together by the bonds of love. His irony is not gone, but his arrogance and hatred must seem to him silly foolishness.

The journalists moved like seaweed, swaying with cameras to right and to left. From my throne I looked at the ' Last Judgment '. Grime and smoke have smirched and blackened those glories, yet the terror of the Judgment remains. Stendhal, in his Journal, one hundred and thirty-two years ago, said:

Greek sculpture was unwilling to reproduce the terrible in any shape; the Greeks had enough real troubles of their own. Therefore, in the realm of art, nothing can be compared with the figure of the Eternal drawing forth the first man from nonentity. The pose, the drawing, the drapery, all is striking: the soul is agitated by sensations that are not usually communicated through the eyes. When in our disastrous retreat from Russia, it chanced that we were suddenly wakened in the middle of the dark night by an obstinate cannonading, which at each moment seemed to gain in nearness, then all the forces of a man's nature gathered close around his heart; he felt himself in the presence of fate, and, having no attention left for things of vulgar interest, he made himself ready to dispute his life with destiny. The sight of Michael Angelo's pictures has brought back to my consciousness that almost forgotten sensation. Great souls enjoy their own greatness; the rest of the world is seized with fear, and goes mad.

I rose from my throne and slipped among the journalists to the foot of the ' Last Judgment '. I touched with my finger the figure in the extreme left-hand corner that is said to be Michael Angelo himself. His very hand had painted where my hand rested. A reprehensible act on my part, but I fancied that I felt the warmth of bone and flesh and saw the expanse of dirt-smokened canvas flame to a sudden light of glory and splendour.

My last act was to be photographed with Hillman pushing sticks into the stove that was to hold the fire for the smoke telling the world that a new Pope was elected.

On the following day we all attended to witness the last procession of the Cardinals before they were locked into the Conclave. After many altercations with policemen, showing of tickets, grinning at Swiss Guards, we found ourselves with a select number in a splendid hall that led from the Sistine to another chapel, packed together behind ropes, but very close to the pathway of the procession.

We were a motley crowd of journalists, ladies in black, gentlemen in evening dress, officers in uniform, priests and monks. We were all pressed very tightly together against the rope. Everyone chattered and pushed and laughed. The Noble Guards lined the aisle, and an officer, resplendent in gilt and embroidery, strutted up and down. The hall was magnificently painted with pictures of tremendous battles on sea and land. Behind me was a vast glowing canvas of high ships in flames, men struggling in the water and lurid waves lit at their edges with lightning. Everything glittered and shone. The heat was intense and there was a scent of musk and sweat. I was wedged between two fat priests and pressed upon by another. Although the chatter was of monkeys there was also an air of breathless expectation.

The heat, the thick scent, the pressure upon me of stout bodies created in me a kind of visionary unreality. I have never fainted in my life, but I was perhaps not far from fainting now. And yet I felt no weakness; although my hand was pushed against the fat thigh of the priest next to me I felt no desire for his support or, indeed, anyone's.

It was rather as though I had been translated into another world and that an evil one. I was somewhere in a place of glittering richness and the thick enervating scent of hot-house flowers. I saw the cartoon on the wall behind me quite clearly, but it seemed to move as though the figures in the sea were alive, I could almost hear their cries. The men and women pressing in upon me were real and not real. Certain journalists I had learnt by this time to know by sight, and I can remember a tall thin man with pince-nez and hair *en brosse*, the elegant Englishman representing *The Times* and my own Frank Gervasi with his restless vitality and kindliness. I remember, too, the thick plump body of the priest against whom I was, willy-nilly, pressing, the thick red rolls of flesh at the back of his neck, the double chin, the sleepy half-closed eyes. All these were real in their actuality, but they were also figures in some play or pageant or masque. In this masque I too was performing and it was a part evil and sensuous. I not only acquiesced in this part but was glad of it. And, as in *John Inglesant* at the court of the Duke of Umbria, so I seemed to look on to a whirling tangle of lascivious figures and know that in a moment or two I also would join the dance and, dancing, lose my integrity.

This fantasy must seem exaggerated at this later time, but the consciousness of splendid and rewarding evil was not exaggerated. I remember that something within myself, as though I were in a dream, said: " You have, through all these months, been fighting your way to the centre. Now you are there; and it is not God that you have found but the Devil." For the Devil is very real, at certain times, to anyone with imagination.

It was as in a dream that I heard the singing of the choir in the distance, saw the Noble Guard stand at salute and, at the same time, felt the whole loggia crammed with figures that were other than my own immediate companions. We were pressed in with witnesses and they were not the Saints of God.

Leaning against the rope as the procession passed I could, by stretching out my hand, have touched any of the members. First came the choir-boys and the priests, then the Cardinals. There were over sixty of them and the majority wore their splendid crimson. They advanced slowly and around me, on every side, was the buzz of names. But I was more than ever in my dream and these were figures in it. Their faces were to me then like a page of grotesques drawn by Leonardo; and their bodies only bodies — fat ones, tall ones, thin ones, short ones. And of the faces I saw so very few that were holy — three or four at the most. Holy? I didn't wish them to be holy, and that was why I saw them as I did, for it is in ourselves that truth or falsehood lies.

It was a procession of grotesques, of phantasmagoria. Protruding chins, two, three, four chins, no chins at all, dented chins, bony chins, short noses, long noses, nostrils distended, nostrils tight and pinched, eyes staring and vapid, little eyes like dead pebbles, big staring eyes like those of glazed fish, bright burning lustful eyes, eyes of cold intelligence, and mouths tight and thrifty, mouths thick and sensual, mouths slack and aimless. All these within myself, created by me, hemmed in on every side by the masque of the decorated ghosts, by the dead who were living, and the living so nearly dead. One of these moving past me would soon be Pope, would have the destiny of nearly half the civilized world in his hands.

They moved into the further chapel and we heard the singing of the Mass. Through the hot sick disgust, miasmic and revolting, of myself I was conscious for a moment of the room at Castel Gandolfo and the Astronomer saying, " He would often have his meal here — fruit and cheese — and he would look at the charts of the stars while he was eating."

They were returning. I felt a vast, devastating depression. I had come all this way and this was all that I had found — I did not care who would be Pope. My body was sweating, in my nostrils a thick sweet stench, and in my heart a sad longing for any libertinage. I had come all this way to find only evil.

The procession had stopped, and so close to me that my hand could most easily close on his long thin arm was Pacelli, the late Pope's secretary. I had seen so many photographs of him that he did not seem a stranger. I knew that many thousands of men and women longed for him to be elected. It was the common rule that anyone who had been secretary to the last Pope could not be the new Pope, for it was always expected that, with the new Pope, there would be a fresh, original policy. I had heard many things for him, some things against him. He was very much more of a world-diplomat than Pius XI could ever have been. Not so simple a man. He was this and he was that.

Now, as I looked at him, standing so close to me, his thin beautiful fingers pressed together, his large brilliant eyes lost in his vision, his powerful lips moving in prayer, I forgot anything I had ever heard. It was as though he turned to me and with one quick gesture threw off from me all my burden of evil.

He did not, of course, turn or move. I have no wish to exaggerate. The confused evil un-happiness, the eagerness to surrender to temptation, the sense of many abnormal spirits driving in upon me during the last half-hour had been very real, not at all sentimentally imagined. Wishing to speak the truth and the truth only, I can but say that I was in contact, at this moment, quite suddenly, with a goodness and a spiritual integrity that I could not doubt any more than I could doubt the reality of the tortoiseshell spectacles upon the thick nose of the priest next to me.

Dramatically, and perhaps falsely, I might say that Pacelli's eyes shone with a fire of purpose, with a humility and with a spiritual power that I had seen in no man's eyes before. But the ecstatic vision in that face was no histrionic falsity. It was his relation to myself, although he did not know that I was there, and would never know, that lifted my burden so gloriously for me. ' Go down into Sodom and find one righteous man. It is enough.' I had gone down and I had found him.

He moved forward at last and it was as though I moved with him.

This was on March 1st.

On March 2nd I got up very early and hustled along to our Hearst Hiding-hole. About this something must be said.

Ever since Frank Gervasi had arrived in Rome from America he and Bill Hillman had had but one thought between them — namely, how could they get the name of the newly-elected Pope to the outside world before anyone else? This was not so easy. As everyone knows, the stove, into which Hillman and I had been photographed pushing sticks, led to a chimney and the chimney stretched up through the Sistine Chapel into the open sky. So soon as any Cardinal received two-thirds of the votes at any meeting of the Conclave a thin white smoke issued into the sky from the chimney, and the whole world was certain that a new Pope had been elected. There were two meetings every day, and therefore twice every day — at twelve and at five — smoke would issue from the chimney. When there was no election the smoke would be black.

So much for the smoke. But there was more in it for us than this. For about an hour after the smoke was perceived the identity of the new Pope would still be a secret, would be a secret indeed until an official appeared on the window-balcony of St. Peter's and proclaimed the name. After that there would again be a pause while the new Pope arrayed himself in a white robe — white dresses of three sizes were held in readiness — before appearing in front of his people.

For Gervasi, therefore, two things were necessary. He must, in one way or another, know that it was *white* smoke before anyone else, and secondly he must have some secret information, before anyone else, as to the identity of the new Pope. As to the second of these I did not know then, I do not know now, anything at all, but our preparations for the seeing of the smoke were as romantic and decorative as *The Castle of Otranto* or *The Mysteries of Udolpho*.

Gervasi rented a priests' chapel and lodging-house exactly opposite St. Peter's, or rather one room in the lodging-house. This was a little house, as it might be a hiding-place in any spy story or romantic novel. Outside it was innocent enough, a shabby house with a shabby door and in front of it a ruin of stones and rubble where some houses had been destroyed to further Mussolini's plans for a great wide road to St. Angelo.

Passing through the shabby little door you found yourself climbing some rough stairs to-wards a room full of ugly Madonnas and crucifixes and paper flowers, a room that was for some reason being repainted. Down a passage on the left was a kitchen, and this place fascinated me because it was human and lively, and hugged, with enjoyment, an enchanting smell of good cooking. I would look through the doorway and see a stout priest, his sleeves turned up, rocking pans over a slow fire, absorbed and contented.

Roman Fountain

Up some more stairs you came to the narrow bedrooms of the priests, and it was one of these bedrooms that we had hired. The room was incongruously filled. In the middle of it was a large telescope turned exactly on the slender chimney rising above the Vatican roofs. There was a bed; there was a tin washing-stand; there was a picture of Madonna and Child above the bed. There was a table with telephones, a wireless and a typewriter, a sofa and a chair.

Into this we all crowded, Michael grinning, Noyes kindly and amiable as always, Gervasi as excited as though we were about to discover, once and for ever, that there was life on Mars, and myself with a Dante and a Penguin detective story to fill in time if nothing occurred.

Opposite us, in full and perfect view, were St. Peter's, the Square and the Vatican, and, at first, on that fine morning, the only life was composed of the pigeons, of a few loiterers, a taxi or two, a procession of priests and some tourists with a gesticulating guide. But, looking through the telescope, the fatal chimney was as brilliant and dramatic as the pointing finger of fate. I had it driven deep into my soul that if I were not the very first human being in the world to see the white smoke wheedling its way through that chimney I had failed in the whole purpose of my journey to Rome.

There had been much discussion as to how long this Conclave would last. There had been historic Conclaves that had lasted for months. There had been one such, I remembered, in *John Inglesant*. So long as the Conclave lasted I was a prisoner there. The authorities, however — those who really knew — said that this one would be short. The seriousness of the international situation demanded a new Pope as soon as possible. A week perhaps? Yes, possibly, a week. Gervasi, however, thought that, at the very most, it would be three days.

The morning began slowly and rightfully to swallow itself. Now only Gervasi and I were in the priest's bedroom. Michael was posted in the Square, beneath one of the pillars. From this position he could see the man on the wall opposite the chimney who would get a vision of the smoke before anyone in the Square. He would wave a hand to Michael, who would wave a hat to Gervasi, who would instantly telephone to New York.

I stared through the telescope at the chimney. The radio was turned on and, in a cultured Oxford accent, was spilling out German propaganda:

" The Führer's love for all Germans wherever they may be, in the lost plains of China or in the darkest depths of Africa, cannot surely be abused by any lover of truth.   That his heart should go out to those exiled sons . . ."

At this moment Gervasi's own personal telephone sounded. He listened. I heard him say: " Christ, but it can't be true! Where did he see the notices? Send Garibaldi down. . . . Maybe he didn't read them right. . . . What! you say everyone's excited? Crowds gathering? Send Garibaldi down. . . . Yes.   Pronto."

He turned round to me, his brown face puckered like a monkey's, his eyes glittering.

" War! "

" What! "

" Yes. . . . Oh, hell . . . it can't be.   But it must be.   They've called up all the reservists. Notices up all down the Corso."

I stared through the telescope.   It was half-past eleven.

" Big crowds now."

" They'll be bigger when they hear this news."

He was dictating messages through to London and New York.   Then I heard his sharp cry:

" What!   Only those years? . . . Why, that means nothing.   They call them up in the natural

. . . Wait till I get to him to wring his bloody neck. . . ."

He turned round nonchalantly to me.

" It's only those two classes. . . . What the hell! . . . Getting me all het up . . . ! "

My eye was still in the telescope — but, deep in my soul, I realized a curious thing. I had moved on, past hysteria. On that Tuesday evening of the Munich September, the Botts staying with me in Brackenburn, I had, at that last late 11.40 broadcast, turned to them and said:

" Yes. This really *is* War. This really *is* War! "

And Alan, looking at me in that half-alive, wholly-intelligent, indifferent spirit of his, said, with all the genius of divine prophecy, " Mussolini is the only man who can do anything now."

But I did then (and it was the only time) sink deep, deep into the waters of despair. I raged up and down the room crying out on the folly, the madness, the insane crime. . . . But beneath and behind these cries was the certain sure knowledge that France and ourselves were utterly unprepared. I happened to know, from some chance information, that our defence of London simply didn't exist. I foresaw as inevitable the most ghastly massacre of human beings in modern history, a possible panic submission, and so, after all, that world rule of force and tyranny, that nightmare to the freedom of mankind.

I admired and even loved the Czechs, but with that vision in front of me I would have readily sacrificed the Czechs to save the world — for they would, in any case, have been sacrificed with the rest of us. On the following day Neville Chamberlain did save the world.

This, however, is most certainly not a book of politics. I record this only because, during that lively moment when Gervasi moved into world war and out of it again, I knew that the panic of September 1938 was over, as far as Englishmen were concerned, for ever. Hitler should have struck then. During the months that followed we recovered our force, our balance, our confidence, our firm resolve.

" As there isn't going to be a war just now I think I'll go down into the Square."

I went down, stood beside Michael and watched. Twelve o'clock struck and shortly afterwards the smoke came out. The first curl or two seemed as white as Bernard Shaw's beard, but it darkened, it darkened. . . . Everyone sighed and turned away home.

I had a curious unnatural feeling that it was my fault that the smoke was black. Nay, worse than that, the wrong Pope would be chosen and I should be to blame. The whole world would be ruined (was it not hanging on the edge of ruin?) and it would be my fault. I had not discovered my Fountain. The Fountain was illusion. I was an ass and a sentimental, romantic, imagining-where-there-is-nothing kind of ass to boot. It is when I am tempted towards the realists that I am most miserable. Jack Priestley, for whom I would do almost anything, thinks he sees exactly what is what and that I never can. I write an article about Freedom. He says it's a good article but not at all about Freedom.

" My kind of Freedom."

" There's only one sort of Freedom."

" You want men to be free but have poor hopes of them. But I have good hopes of them whether they are free or no. I'm more of an ass than you about the ground I'm standing on, but wiser in taking a long view."

He won't admit that, of course, and I remember that, at this moment, as I went with my Dante and my Penguin under my arm to the restaurant in the corner of the Square, I thought of him, longed for his company as I so often do, and felt he was right about everything. This is a bad world. Men are such fools. They will elect a wicked Pope. That is the way the world is going now. And over my macaroni I saw the burning eyes of Pacelli darkening in sorrow. Out of the sunny gloom from the pillars the four friends I had made in Rome came towards me — Michael Angelo Buonarroti the sculptor, Keats the poet, Pius XI the mountainclimber, Pacelli the friend of God and of man. I was cheered. They seemed so close to me and so happy. Had Jack Priestley been with me I would have introduced him. They are exactly the kind of men he likes. The trouble with him is that his standards are so dreadfully high.

But while I ate my luncheon I reflected, as I suppose hundreds of thousands in Rome on that day were reflecting, that the Cardinals, shut in there, seated each one under his canopy and under the brilliant imaginings of Michael Angelo, were intriguing and scheming and moving, as in a game of chess, from one position to another. How near had anyone been, at that first meeting this morning, to a required majority? Had parties by now been formed behind this candidate and that? The disgust remained with me.

I was unhappy during all that afternoon. Perhaps the false alarm that morning about the war had distressed me more deeply than I knew. The crowds began to gather again and they looked so innocent, so friendly, so humble, so eager to be good and to love their fellow-men.

The Italian, when he is not disturbed by any violent passion, is the most amiable of all mankind. He wants no trouble with anyone. He does not see why everything should not be perfectly all right to the end of time. An English crowd is as good-tempered as any, but there is a lack of imagination at the heart of it. It also is kindly, ready to be friendly, wanting only the best for everyone, but it is tepid about all humankind who are not English, tepid in understanding and a little pitying. But these Italians, now, many of them monks and priests, were waiting on a world-event and were praying for the whole Universe. All civilization was within their embrace, now, on this blue-gilt afternoon, looking steadfastly at the dove-coloured façade of St. Peter's.

And I thought how awful it would be if aeroplanes, possibly from my own country, silently came up and smashed them as they stood there. They would not, in actual fact, be standing there and waiting, but thousands of Chinese, only in the last month, had been smashed in just that fashion, and in Barcelona children had run across the squares, screaming . . .

I wanted, in fact, passionately that those en-

closed Cardinals should do something that would
help to save the world — that they choose a man
who would, in his own time and fashion, be God's
man. What happened in this Election would
weigh the balance towards Salvation or Destruction.
It appeared to me, as I crossed the sun-splashed
Square, that the consequence of this event was
heavy with importance. I was impotent. We
were all impotent. Those Cardinals in the
Sistine . . .

And then, shortly after four o'clock, I left the
Square and went back to the city office. It was
a lazy, slack thing to do and showed that I was
not really a good journalist. But Gervasi, tele-
phoning at his table, said that he thought it unlikely there would be a decision tonight.

I went into the café under the office and sat
there drinking a cup of coffee, and watched a
stout man with little eyes in a crimson face making
love to a stout lady with a brown Pekinese dog.
He leant over her with that urgency that elderly
men have when they make love — as though there
was little time to lose. His short fat fingers hung
just above her fine bosom and stirred and wavered
like antennae. He was gazing hard at her stomach
and murmuring, murmuring, while she stared
about her, looking at one person after another

with an air of vast satisfaction, as much as to say to everybody, " I'm not as young as I was but I can still rouse passion in a man."

I thought how very stout they both were and how kindly God is to ageing human beings, if they will only be patient and not lose their heads. Then I looked again and saw, to my amazement, that this was Mr. Garside! Preoccupied with his affections, he appeared, physically and spiritually, a new creature. Terrified lest he should find me spying upon him, I laid my coin on the little table and hurried away.

I went, at a leisurely pace, up the dark staircase and wandered into the office. As I passed the door I saw Hillman swerve towards me. He screamed (yes, he screamed!):

" A Pope is elected! A Pope is elected! Go back! Go back! "

XVI

I TURNED, I flashed down the stairs, stumbling, gasping, risking my neck in that half-gloom, pushed out into the twisting pattern of Italians, grasped a taxi by its mane, shouted " St. Peter's " to the driver and hung on to the window, praying that I might be in time.

In time for what? I didn't quite know. After the smoke there was, of course, an interval before the name of the new Pope was announced. That name had, in all probability, been already telephoned by Gervasi to New York and if I hurried to the little priests' house I should learn it.

But, oddly enough, I didn't want to see Gervasi or the priests' house or anything to do with any newspaper. I was dimly aware that at some time

that evening I should have to send an account of
this Election to America, but I wasn't thinking of
that now.

All I wanted was to be with the crowd at
St. Peter's. I repeated aloud to myself over and
over again, " In time. . . . In time . . ." The
kind of chump I'd been to miss the white smoke
after all! But it didn't seem now to be the
important thing — the important thing was that I
should be there when they announced the name of
the new Pope.

We were level with the priests' house when
the taxi stopped. The crowd had stopped it.
From here, some quarter of a mile from St. Peter's,
a vast, packed, unstirring crowd stretched to the
foot of the church. Heads, heads, unmoving,
staying as though in a trance — a stagnant lake of
heads up to the very walls of the church.

I plunged into it and, very strangely, it opened
wherever I pressed. There was no resistance — I
had not to murmur a ' Prego '. I was to see one
other vast crowd in Rome before the end and that
was to be in spirit and temper very different from
this. This was, in fact, a quite new crowd in my
experience. In all probability I shall never see
another like it. As it parted so easily before me
I moved, like a man swimming, almost to the

bottom of the steps leading up to the great doors. There was a line of soldiers here.

I stopped and stayed, and looked forward to the balcony in front of the window where the announcer of the name of the new Pope would stand. I was aware, then, in the silence that was on every side of me, of a tense, an almost agonizing anxiety.

It was not only that priests on every side of me were praying, not only that, in all those eyes staring at the window high and far away, there was a beseeching, an imploring expression — there was also a tenseness, the sense in the air above us and around us of thousands upon thousands of souls beseeching God for something; the Israelites must have been thus when they waited for the rain to fall from heaven. Beside me was a young priest from the American College.

" There was no mistake, was there? " I asked. " It was the white smoke that came out."

" Oh yes. It was the white smoke all right," he answered, grinning.

" Was it white from the start? "

" It was like a puff of cigarette smoke. That's what it was — cigarette smoke. It went wriggling up — grey at first, quite white at the end."

" Were you surprised? "

" Oh yes. Of course we were. They said it would be three or four days. I'm afraid it won't be Pacelli."

" Why not? "

" Yes. It must be Pacelli," another American boy broke in quite furiously. " Don't you know they said that if he was going to be elected it would be in the first two days? After that he would have no chance. Well, here it is . . . the very first day. . . ."

" All right. I know. But Pacelli hasn't all that following, you know. The politicians . . ."

Pacelli. Pacelli. Pacelli. Everywhere I heard the name breathed. It hung in the air as though the wishes of all those hearts were vocal.

Above that sea of heads the sky was turning a white-green like the pale curve of a centuries-washen bowl. I gazed round me as though I were seeing Bernini's wonderful Square for the first time, and it was an absolute truth that I had never seen it like this before. History was once again being made in it. That old, old obelisk brought by Caligula to Rome, which has reached our generation intact — what horrors of orgies and bloody games it has seen! — the bony fanatic Christians dressed in skins and devoured by wild dogs (the first hot breath, stinking, of the dogs upon the withdrawn cheek!), the living torches, for Nero to bite his nails to the quick in restless pleasure, the actual crucifixion and death of St. Peter, at last its removal by Sixtus V from in front of the sacristy to this centre of the Square, where it became of all ironies Christian, and has been venerated by millions of pilgrims from 1586 until now.

I looked at this old obelisk and watched the kindly gentle faces stretching from side to side of the Square. Cruelty of man to man, how strange, how illogical — for we are a freak, a ' sport ' from Nature's pattern. We are Nature and something very much more as well. For us to return to Nature, as the cry of the poets and philosophers once was, is to go back altogether on our tracks, to return to the living torches lighting ruddily the writing on the obelisk. There can be no return.

On every side of me they began to sing a psalm in sombre-measured Gregorian. Next to me, his face raised under his black felt hat, his mouth smiling, was a young ruddy-faced priest. He seemed little more than a boy. He had the shoulders of a prize-fighter. He was singing and smiling, both at the same time. Next to him was a long, tall, towering monk, thin, fanatic.

His lips were moving in prayer, his large coarse-skinned hands raised, clasped together. I have seldom seen so strained, so acute a sense of anxiety in any face.

The sound of the singing grew stronger and stronger. It was picked up and enforced on the very outskirts of the crowd. Pink streamers of cloud floated into the pale green sky as though someone were hanging out banners.

The singing stopped. A figure appeared on the balcony. What a stillness that was! The whole of Rome, nay, the world beyond it, was stilled. The little boy-priest caught my sleeve with his hand. I could feel the beat of his heart against my side. He was staring forward as though he would *force* truth from the Universe. Somewhere in that vast crowd a baby cried and was instantly hushed.

The voice of the man on the balcony came with happy freshness — you could feel how joyful he was. He said, in Latin, " I am happy to tell you that we have once again a Pope. . . ." He said some more words. Then, isolating it from the surrounding words, the name — " Pacelli."

Oh! what a roar broke out then, what a shout, what a cry! " Pacelli! Pacelli! Pacelli! "

And to show his kinship with Pius XI, whom

he had dearly loved, he would himself be
' Pius XII '.

" Pacelli! Pacelli! Pacelli! " I found that I
myself was crying. I, who was no Catholic, who
had seen Pacelli but once, to whom this must
surely be an outside affair, was joyfully happy as
though my dear friend had received his heart's
desire. I felt it so personally that I had to speak
to the young priest: " I *am* so glad. That makes
me so happy. *Now* things will be better. . . ."
And he, knowing no English at all, smiled and
laughed and looked at me as though he loved
me.

Down the furrowed brown cheeks of the tall
monk tears were trickling. He stared in front of
him, rigid, carven. The American priests were
chattering like birds in an aviary.

" That's bully. Who said it wouldn't be
Pacelli? Of course it had to be, the state the
world's in. And he's *clever*. He's a diplomat.
He'll keep the world straight. He's a good man,
too, although he's so clever."

We had to wait, some half-hour or so, while
Pacelli was arrayed in his white robe, and it was
during this half-hour that I participated, for the
second time in my life, in the conscious, active,
glorious happiness of the Brotherhood of Man.

Roman Fountain

I remember that, at that very moment, I said to myself: " I must drink this deep into my spirit. I must realize that this is happening — truly and actually happening, and that, whatever things of hatred and terror the future holds, this also is true."

I have said something already, I think, of those days at the beginning of the March Revolution in Petrograd in 1917 when we all walked along the streets, arm in arm, singing, loving one another, and, what is more, *trusting* one another. So it was now. For half an hour three hundred thousand of us stood, hand in hand as it were, joyful and happy, believing in God, believing in Peace, and *trusting one another*.

Had we who stood there been given the ruling of the world, and *stayed permanently in the spirit and temper that we then experienced*, there would be no more fighting, no more lust of selfishness and cruelty of desire. For an instant, believing in God, being willing to put His precepts into practice, we saw clearly, we knew the only Law:

Jesus said unto him, Thou shalt love the Lord thy God with all thy heart, and with all thy soul, and with all thy mind. This is the first and great commandment. And the second is like unto it, Thou shalt love thy neighbour as thyself. On these two commandments hang all the Law and the Prophets.

At that single moment of time it seemed ridiculously easy. Love God? Love your neighbour? Why, of course, what is there to prevent it? Let us all share and share alike. Let us meet in a World Conference and say: " What do *you* want? What are *your* needs? . . . Certainly you can have that piece, even more if you like it. And instead of bombs let us make new schools with shower-baths and halls of song.

Everyone was singing again. The stars were breaking into the sky.

The thin white figure appeared on the balcony. All we, his children, received his blessing.

XVII

THE Election was on March 2nd. The Coronation was to be held on March 12th. Ten days. My birthday was on March 13th. On March 13th I would be fifty-five years of age. I had intended to spend it with Harold in Naples. Now I would spend it alone. I had not been alone on my birthday for thirty years.

It seemed to me, however, a symbolical and amazing portent that this Roman adventure should end on the very day before my birthday. Not symbolical for anyone else, of course, but one more piece of evidence as to the extraordinary nature of my history.

Is this vanity, conceit, egotism? I don't know. It seems to me that without thinking yourself wonderful you may yet think your existence wonderful. That I emerged from my mother's womb with five perfect fingers on one hand seems to me wonderful enough. In any case I now had ten days in which to prepare for the climax. Or perhaps the climax had already occurred? I should only know when I looked back on the whole of it. I had ten days in which to find the Fountain.

I have always known the exquisite pleasure of tasting things on my tongue. When I bought my ' White ' Utrillo (I bought it in a passion of excitement one morning from my friend Dick Smart in the little back room at Tooth's: bought it when I could ill afford it, having a dreadful income-tax to pay that very month and the future desperately uncertain for every literary man) Dick Smart and I took it and hung it over the mantelpiece in the flat, and I sat down and looked at it, and saw twelve contrasted whites in it of such loveliness that my heart constricted. It was like falling in love. I don't say that it is the best Utrillo in the world, but I do say that there is none better anywhere.

Well, for weeks after hanging it there I would suddenly in the middle of a meal, or waking at three in the morning, or trying to write an article, or walking home through the débris of Curzon

Roman Fountain

Street of an evening when the gentlemen's gentlemen are taking the dogs for a walk and the ladies are clustered about the corner of Half Moon Street hoping to make a new friend — I would suddenly think of that picture, hanging there, lighting the dusk of the room with its warm whiteness, or sparkling like snow in the sunshine, or thick and deep, white upon white upon white, and I would know an instant pang of happiness, a conscious active pang with gratitude in it for my lucky life, and humility before great beauty, and pathos because soon, as time goes, I would be dead.

In this way, too, I have carried in my pocket my awareness of a friendship, of a lovely scene like the tide coming in off the rocks below Tregarthen's, of a passage in Montaigne or Proust, Cervantes or Wordsworth, of the Second Movement in the Seventh Beethoven, or a certain Schumann Quartette, of Chaliapin in *Prince Igor*, or Denis Compton driving to the boundary at Lord's. How possibly can life not be lovely in spite of war, disease, poverty, betrayal?

So now I felt about Rome. I had been there long enough, had surrendered myself sufficiently to carry it now with me, a tapestry of pillar and fountain, of dull amber wall and a church door, of the trees of the Borghese, the valley of Rome

from the Janiculum, the flowers against the
Spanish Steps, the headless dancing girl in the
National Museum, the brown and gold primitive
of Francescuccio Ghissi in the Vatican picture-
gallery, the Praxiteles Faun in the Capitoline
Museum, Michael Angelo's Moses, the Ephebus
of Subiaco — all caught and held as one entity
by me, going with me for the rest of my time.

The happiness that had descended upon me
on that evening of the Election remained with me.
I think it stayed with many others who were
there, and I fancy that, all through Rome, some
consciousness of it was felt by everyone during
those few days.

I had not to write any articles. Now that
Pacelli was elected no more interest was felt by
the outside world in these events except in the
details of the Coronation. I went to a revue with
Hillman and Gervasi and was surprised at the light
but friendly mockery of Mussolini; I attended a
football match between Rome and another town
and was surprised at the bad quality of the football; I went with Alfred Noyes to some museums
and churches and delighted in his company; I
drank wine with Hilaire Belloc. But, in reality,
quietly and without saying anything to anybody,
I searched for my Fountain.

Roman Fountain

First I thought that there might be something in my novels about Rome to help me. I was to find the Fountain through the light of my imagination. The novelists also had searched Rome with imagination. They might guide me.

They were a mixed lot: Hawthorne's *Transformation*, Crawford's *Saracinesca*, James' *Daisy Miller*, Zola's *Rome*, Shorthouse's *John Inglesant*, Corvo's *Hadrian the Seventh*. I am not going to discuss or compare them here. Indeed, I was not considering them now, at all, from any literary point of view. They were the reactions of imaginative artists to the spirit of a place and I thought that I might find somewhere in their pages an experience parallel with my own.

As a work of *art* only one of these novels can be seriously considered. *Daisy Miller* is a perfect provincial work of art. It is not universal but New England, and Daisy herself is perfection as Elizabeth in *Pride and Prejudice*, Lucy Snowe in *Villette*, Rosamond Vincy in *Middlemarch* are perfect. But Rome in *Daisy Miller* is provincial — the Colosseum is drawn into the rays of the New England moon.

Marion Crawford I have already written about sufficiently in this book. His Rome would be altogether of the theatre did he not know it so well and love it so dearly. The Rome for which I was searching was not there, any more than the lady of the little shop so many years ago, who had made me think of him, was a Roman.

Zola also in *his Rome* was no artist. When he wrote that book he had reached the stage in his life when he saw Zola everywhere. This did not mean that he was conceited, although he *was* conceited. It meant that he saw himself no longer as a comic creature. So he wrote *Évangiles*. The story-climax of Zola's *Rome*, is perhaps the most absurd in any novel anywhere — the moment when the naked heroine throws herself on the corpse of the dead hero and at last surrenders her virginity to him. Obscene and horrible it would have been in the hands of Poe, or even Henry James.

Nevertheless Zola's *Rome* is not only a guide-book. The agonies of the poor persecuted little Abbé and, at last, his interview with the Pope, are moving and even poignant. But the Rome I searched for was not here.

Corvo's *Hadrian the Seventh* is a fantasy and a very brilliant one. It contains the best account of a Pope's Election and Coronation in any literature. There pervades it, however, an intense egoistic dissatisfaction, and you feel that Corvo's cruel, pathetic, touching, savage, self-pitying, wildly creative being would not have been fulfilled even had he been the Pope himself.

When Hawthorne wrote *Transformation*, *or The Marble Faun*, he made himself his own taskmaster as George Eliot did when she laboured at *Romola*. The two books have much in common, although I can re-read *Romola* and shall never look at *Transformation* again. Whatever may be the right way to create novels of Place, it is certainly the *wrong* way to guide-book them.

Yet through all the descriptions of monuments and customs and costumes there peeps ever and again the shy, suspicious, priggish eye of genius that was Hawthorne's. The personality of few literary men in history makes me more uncomfortable, and never will I forgive him his chilly unintelligence, bred of prudery and fear, when the great Herman Melville, in a worship of friendliness, came close to him and asked for his affection. Nevertheless there is genius in this book — even as the sun falls in glittering stars and moons upon the mud flats of Galloway when the tide is out.

No, of all these novels only one has anything of the spirit of true Rome, and that is *John Inglesant*. But Shorthouse, who wrote that book, never went to Rome in his life.

Roman Fountain

Edmund Gosse, rather unkindly, wrote an article once which proved that Shorthouse took all the Italian landscape in the second half of his novel out of books — the Election of the Pope and the ceremonies of the Coronation also. Very shocking. But oddly enough it does not matter in the least. In any actual sense of the word Shorthouse was no novelist, although I will always put in a plea for that queer little book *The Little Schoolmaster Mark*. What he was was a Puritan with an intense awareness of Evil. *John Inglesant* lives, and will always live for certain persons in every generation, because it is a crystal-pure, simple-hearted statement of one man's mysticism. Inglesant lives, not because he is Inglesant, but because he is the inner Shorthouse. The tapestries of Little Gidding, Italian hills and roads, Italian mist-encompassed villas, Rome, hang in sombre folds behind a human soul in pursuit of its enemy who is the other part of itself.

It does not matter that the descriptions of Rome are borrowed. These Roman streets and buildings are charged with that struggle between good and evil, that supreme effort to rise to the high, pure upper light above the plague marshes, that must always seem to some men and women the supreme task of this earthly life. Shorthouse believed this with all his heart and soul, and so he made his Rome universal. Therefore his was the only book that, during the weeks before the Coronation, helped me in my search.

And here I would like to repeat what I said at the beginning of this book, that my search was not whimsical nor mystical nor in any way fantastic.

At the beginning of this Roman visit I had not the slightest doubt but that, in a moment of time, I would come on my Fountain. It was as real to me as I was to myself, that is, half real. The only complete reality I have ever known in my life has been in a world spiritual as well as physical, which is why I am sure in my own mind that there is a reality beyond my intelligence and only to be touched by my *mind*. My *brain* is powerless to grasp it, which is the reason why brain alone, isolated, has never roused my very strong admiration. Einstein, Whitehead, Frazer are mystics — Shaw also. But Wells falls short because his only remedies as well as his explanations are brain-remedies. Why the words, movements, aspirations of Hitler have seemed to me, from the beginning, scarecrow-stuffed-straw (disastrous though they may easily be in their results) is because the only real world of growth and experience is ignored by them. From

Socrates, Jesus, St. Francis, all the *true* movements have come, and from their successors, followers, disciples, all *true* progress continues.

I perceived, then, now what I had not perceived when I first arrived in Rome, that my life, from now onwards, must really be spent in separating the important from the unimportant. It might even *not* be important that myself and all my generation should be wiped out by war. A poem by Auden (although I do not think him as yet a great poet), a sonata by Benjamin Britten, a painting by young Moynihan, a woman's speech at a County Council meeting, the completion of a rockery at Brackenburn — any one of these and a thousand, thousand more might be of more importance than *all* destruction because they were acts of creation. Only the positive deed, created by love (love whether of God, person, beauty, humanity), counted. . . .

I knew that I put this new realization of creation against destruction badly to myself. My brain has been always a muddled, sentimentalized, limited, ill-trained affair. But the truth of the persistence and progress of creation — its unceasing spiritual life — and therefore the grandeur and splendour of existence whatever the destroying cancer or the devouring flame — this was no less a truth because it has been apprehended by a mentally inferior creature.

I searched for my Fountain that week as though I would suddenly find that I had been carrying it in my pocket all the time. I would stand on the Spanish Steps and look down towards the Corso as though there, in front of the English Tea House, I would find it throwing up its waters.

I went three or four times that week into the narrow close room where Keats died. I only stood there and looked at his handwriting. I envied Severn terribly.

I went on one of these evenings alone to the cinema and saw the *Seven Dwarfs* again, and it was while I was there, during one of the intervals, that I saw Michael Angelo sitting quite close to me, the Michael Angelo of the statue by Antonio Novelli in the Michael Angelo House in Florence. There he was exactly, with the cropped hair, the bulbous broken nose, the fine, scornful mouth, the wonderful long tapering fingers and the thick strong legs. He was alone and apart in spirit as well as body. I would not have dared to speak to him. A woman and a man came and sat down beside him and he moved very decisively away from them.

Quite suddenly, just before the lights went down, he got up and walked out. As he passed me he crunched a piece of paper in his hand and let it drop. I picked it up. It was an advertisement list from some shop of shirts and pants and collars.

No, I didn't, during those ten days, physically look for the Fountain at all. I was expecting some climax, some discovery. . . . I hoped that I was to have, like Saul on the road to Damascus, a revelation.

XVIII

IT wasn't the Coronation that provided it. It would be easy, I suppose, to fake the Coronation, to provide a thundering, screaming blare of trumpets, to fall in wondering obeisance before the new Pope, to close in a whirl of triumphant glory.

The event was quite otherwise. On the Saturday evening preceding it I had my last little talk with Mr. Garside. On the next morning I must rise at five-thirty and once again appear shabbily under the morning sun in evening dress. Mr. Garside was also going to bed early, for he had a ticket. Very fine and starched he was, in spats and dark blue suit and the face of a complacent town-councillor. *Could* it have been *he* in that restaurant?

" Funny the fuss these people are making about their Coronation! "

" *We* made a fuss about *our* Coronation," I said, smiling.

" Oh, well, of course — but that's different. I'll be glad to be home again."

I could see a certain anxiety at the corners of his mouth, and his eyelids, like Mona Lisa's, were weary.

" How have you found the Italians in general? "

He looked around him to be sure that we were safe from spies.

" An odd lot. What is there about a foreigner that makes him so different from an Englishman? "

" Not *being* an Englishman, I suppose."

I asked him whether he had had any chance of meeting Italian ladies.

He shot me a quick glance. Then he looked roguish, which didn't suit him.

" Oh, well, you know what it is."

" How do you find them? "

" I'm a married man — and happily married, too. No man's been luckier than I have. I showed you photos of the family, didn't I? Yes, I thought I had. To tell you the truth, all foreign women are the same — a bit coarse, if you take me. No refinement."

But he looked unhappy. He looked lost, bewildered, even betrayed. I thought that he was about to confide in me. But he didn't. Englishmen never speak to other Englishmen of their sex life.

His face lightened. He smiled proudly.

" The more I'm abroad the more I'm glad I'm an Englishman."

" Why is that? " I asked him.

He seemed a little surprised.

" Surely it's evident enough. We are worth three of any foreigner."

" Do you think we are? "

He stared at me suspiciously. I knew what he was thinking. " Another of these fellows ratting on their own country." And " These writing fellows — never sound."

" Of course I think we are. We're honest for one thing. And clean minded."

" I don't know. Everyone's nasty-minded one time and another. Of course I'm glad I'm English, but the world has changed. I think we've got to see the other man's point of view more. We aren't quick enough or clever enough——— "

" Oh, if you want us to be like the Nazis——— "

" I don't in the least. For one thing I hate Nationalism, although I'm a patriot. I only want us *not* to think ourselves superior——"

" But we *are* superior."

Then he changed, finding the conversation tiresome. He became the charming, child-like, exiled Briton who longs for his home. Thus he was endearing and honest.

" I tell you what it is — I'm just *aching* to be home again. I want to sit in my own chair and see the roses through the window and ask my girl to play the piano and have a pal come in to play billiards. And I want the *Telegraph* hot and strong at breakfast-time, and to take the train to town with the same men on it there've been for years, and take the wife to a cinema and have a run out in the car on a Sunday afternoon." He stopped abruptly. He was a little ashamed of his sincerity. " I've been here long enough to be tired of spaghetti and wondering whether the man standing near you will report you to the police and the tilt of that chap Ciano's hat and — well, women you want to go to bed with but don't give a damn for."

He held out his hand. " Good night. See you in the morning."

But I never saw him again.

I felt, from the first, on the following morning, that this was an anti-climax. Packed into a car we drove round to the back of the Vatican. There were crowds everywhere — once again men in swords and knee-breeches, in mediaeval costume, in horrible evening-dress, as I myself was, ladies in black mantillas, monks and priests. We all scurried about like ants. This door was the right one for some, that door for others, according to the colour of the tickets. We had Hilaire Belloc with us and, as I consider him the best writer now alive in England, I watched him with pleasure. In his black hat and black cloak he was charming, and he was as crammed with vitality as all the rest of us packed together.

Owing to the quicksilver genius of Michael we had the best kind of tickets, and we sailed in through the central doors and up the great nave as though we had just purchased St. Peter's.

I break off for a moment to consider the strange circumstances under which I am writing the closing pages of this book. On this morning, August 25th, 1939, I am looking out, as I write, on the low muddy flats of the bay beyond Rockcliffe in Galloway. The heavy sulky sun has thunder-light from below dark clouds, and gleams down on the water sliding in over the flats, turning all to a grey phosphorescence. A gull is crying, washing hangs over the tangled garden and no breeze stirs it. A portrait of Michael Angelo, my Japanese mask, my porcelain box, ' Johnny ' from Pompeii, are on the table before me and at my feet is today's copy of *The Times* wherein the Berlin Correspondent says:

The crisis which now exists is regarded here as of the utmost gravity and all preparations are being made for the worst. Today most French residents were evacuated from Germany on orders from Paris, leaving, apart from diplomatic and Consular staffs, only a bare handful of journalists in Berlin. No instructions have yet been received by the British authorities in this respect, but the travel offices were crowded today, chiefly by potential neutrals anxious to leave the Reich, with a sprinkling of French and British. Trains running into Holland and Denmark were crowded, and not a seat was to be had on aeroplanes.

We have here the whole familiar business of August 1914 and September 1938. This time it may well mean that we may be started on the worst war of all history in a day or two's time.

When this book *is* published it will be found, I trust, that nothing that has occurred since it was written has altered, in the slightest, its *point*. That point is that immediate history, however disturbing and horrible, does not affect at all the life of the spirit. This book is an honest record of the moments when the writer, not a very spiritual man, perceived the strong, unchecked, rich, glorious undercurrent of the inner, outer, wider, fuller life of the spirit. *That* life immediate current history cannot terminate or destroy although it may influence it.

I do not know how it may be with the world six months or a year from now when this book is published, but I *do* know that the inner life of man will be continuing, richly, rewardingly, often joyfully, as it has always continued, even though London is in ruins and we are living, most of us, on acorns in stout underground cages. I, at this tiresome moment when proud history has seen fit to have its nose tweaked by an Austrian house-painter, confidently salute the future!

Belloc, Michael, Gervasi and I were conducted to a kind of pen immediately opposite the great Baldacchino, with an excellent view of the High Altar and a sweep of the eyes down the centre of the church.

At first I wandered about the pen, pushing and being pushed by a crowd as voluble and noisy as a wilderness of monkeys. The fine thing was to claim a post of vantage where you could see everything even without standing on a chair. The

' standing on a chair ' game was already being played handsomely, the opening moves being to jump upon a chair, to pretend to hear nothing of expostulations until they became so loud that, with an air of sudden surprise, you would jump off again. All this was carried on with the complete knowledge that, once the ceremonies really began, everyone would be standing on chair or bench. The situation created also as pretty an exhibition of temper as I have ever seen.

A very young gentleman in a grey suit and a mackintosh (not, I thought, the ideal costume for a Pope's Coronation) stood like a stork on one leg on a chair, the other cleverly writhed around him. He stood for but a brief while; nevertheless an elderly stout gentleman resembling a minor Savage Landor — choleric, white-haired, cockatoo-beaked — scolded him for his behaviour. The young man said nothing but got off his chair and then surprisingly climbed on again. This infuriated Savage Landor, who shook the chair. The young man, who had been maintaining a strict haughtiness, suddenly turned and abuse (I imagine) flowed from his lips. Savage Landor suitably replied and now they were at it, lip to lip and nose to nose.

It is always exciting to an impassive Englishman

to observe how the body of a Frenchman or Italian gyrates, weaves in and out, heightens and shortens, twists and turns, every feature, every organ obeying its most active orders while the argument lasts. I think I have never seen anyone so angry as Savage Landor seemed to be but quite obviously wasn't, for suddenly, with a shrug of the shoulder, he smiled philosophically and became, in one swift turn of the mind, an amiable poet. Are not the Italians to be loved, whatever the history of the next year may provide? I, writing at this dangerous, absurd moment, say that they are.

I gazed myself out upon a St. Peter's that I had never seen before — for now it was packed from wall to wall, from door to door, with heads that sprouted like black turnip-tops. Immediately opposite and around me, wandering casually, talking, smiling, becking and bowing, were the persons who were now so familiar to me that they were as though I had never spent a day away from them — the white-haired, pinch-nosed official, weak in the hams but covered with decorations (wearing one apparently even on his left ankle), the stout, broad-shouldered, dark-eyed Noble Guard with his thick legs and look of a lazy, amused, but not very intelligent pony, the priests, black-clothed, half-unshaven and with dirty finger-nails, the monks looking strangers in an over-coloured world, looking peasants from the soil, looking on the whole as though they had an inner belief that kept their backs straight. All these were now familiar enough, but never before had I seen St. Peter's filled, like a great white-gilt bowl piled with blackberries.

It altered everything, this vast crowd. This was a public ceremony and almost everything until now, I suddenly realized, had been private. I had come so near to Pius XI and to Pius XII (although the second of these I had seen for only one brief moment) because everything had been private. Now during this Coronation, Pius XI would not be remembered, and Pius XII would be a symbol, not a human being.

I was standing now on my bench, packed close beside two young American priests whose names I will give because they were so kind to me and because they belong to this story. The name of one was Lafferty and the name of the other Carroll, and I hope if either one of them sees this book he will realize that I remember them with affection-ate gratitude.

So together we were standing when the still air was broken with a very moving sound. It was "Papa! Papa! Papa! . . ." and it came from a corner of the church hidden from me.

It was, in the first place, a foreign cry. It had in it an urgency, a plaintiveness and also a shrill joyous excitement. No English people could ever betray their longings so nakedly — their jolly confidence, yes, but not their longings. I knew what it was, for I had already been warned. The Holy Father was being carried in his throne to different places in the church, and each portion of the congregation as he approached it welcomed him.

Suddenly I saw him, a tiny golden image in a golden chair far far away beyond this sea of bobbing black heads, and again I heard the shrill triumphant but also sad cry, " Papa! Papa! Papa! " Now he was an Image. Already I recognized why from the very first I had felt the disappointment — because today my friend who had, it had seemed to me, laid his hand on my shoulder, had vanished behind the image of the Power, the representative of God who spoke from the throne in God's voice, the Power in which I did *not* believe. I believed in the Love but not in the Legend. This did not mean that the Legend was untrue but only that it was untrue for me.

I perceived then that the Pope was coming up through the centre of the great church, and it seemed to me that all the figures in stone, their garments blown by the wind, leaned forward to gaze on this successor in the long line.

And now he was exactly opposite me. The huge Dome was filled with the shouts and cries of everyone around me and opposite me: " Papa! Papa! Papa! " People were hysterical, women waving handkerchiefs. I saw Walter Savage Landor, not angry now, but sobbing, tears rolling down his cheeks. The world around me was blazing with gold. It was exactly contrary to the Funeral, for every light and colour that *could* be used was being used, gold of candles, of garments, even of gold-dust seemed to rise in a heavy incense-dragging cloud into the Dome. The air seemed to my excited eye thick with gold.

He was now close to me. I would like to say here that no photograph that I have seen of Pius XII has given me an impression even remotely resembling him as I saw him on that day of the opening of the Conclave. The photographs represent him as sharp-eyed behind his glasses, a quick-witted, bony ecclesiastic. Now, as I watched him, the man was lost altogether in his office. Robed in gold, gold on his head, gold over his thin shoulders, seated in his chair of gold, his hand lifted, his little head bowing back and forwards, the two huge Eastern-like fans waving on either side of him, the motley crowd, like some sarcastic picture of the world of men, pressing and pushing around the chair, he was both a symbol and a physically small over-weighted human being.

He vanished behind the great Baldacchino.

There followed then, for I know not how long (it seemed an infinity of time), Masses, low Gregorian singing, sudden screaming falsettos. After a while the Pope himself came to celebrate at the altar of the Baldacchino and I could see his little black head now and again between the huge candlesticks.

But for most of the vast congregation the ceremony had passed away from them. It was, in fact, never to return to myself again.

So I sat down on the bench with my young friends, the American priests, Lafferty and Carroll. Everyone around us was gaily chatting, about domesticities, politics, clothes, food, holidays and scandal. We discussed the Roman Catholic religion. My two young friends had kindness and tolerance and a deep sincerity. They thought me a good deal of a fool, but did their polite best not to show this.

At last Michael appeared. " We must see the crowning," he said.

Roman Fountain

During many years the custom of crowning the Pope outside St. Peter's had been in abeyance. Pius XII had revived it.

Wedged into our pen as we were, it seemed impossible that we should ever find our way out of it. But Michael with his smile, his snake-like agility, his charm, and a mysterious sense he carried about with him that he was engaged on some important private mission, managed things very easily. People simply disappeared from in front of us.

In the aisles on the fringe of the packed congregation there was great liveliness. Ladies were sitting under the stone knees of Apostles and eating their luncheon. Babies were tickling their mothers, and large families were holding voluble councils.

It was supposed that we would be forbidden to leave the church while the ceremony was proceeding. Through the great door and under the arches there was, however, an unprevented exit. And so, standing on the top of the steps, I stared out on to what was perhaps the largest assemblage of human beings I had ever seen. From the point where I stood to the outer reaches of the trees and buildings of the skyline the mass appeared completely unbroken. One would scarcely have

related it to human life had it not been for the
eager faces, the expectancy, the child-like happiness of the men and women immediately in front
of one. There, also, I saw Hilaire Belloc eating
sandwiches and drinking out of a bottle. At once
there was a little group of us — Belloc, Tom
Driberg, Michael, Hillman — all of us on the
edge of the crowd looking up to the balcony
where the new Pope would be.

We drove into the crowd a little more deeply,
and Belloc, waving a sandwich, was plunging into
history for my benefit, explaining how in A.D. 200
in the town of Niconphilia a certain king doing
penance . . . or how among the Angevin kings
there was a prince who . . . or it was a mistake
to suppose because the Rhone river ran to the
right instead of to the left. . . .

It was very hot. He would move out of the
sun. It *was* very hot indeed and I was now once
again tightly wedged between monk and priest,
the monk this time an enormous square man with
a red beard and eyes of the lightest blue.

We were all held together by a great expectation, and I, perhaps, by a lively hope that I would
recover now some of that personal private
' sharing ' that I had known from the beginning
until then.

Roman Fountain

Quite suddenly I felt a quiver run through the crowd as the finger of the breeze runs through the corn. At that moment instantly I was aware of a great danger, of the insecurity of all stable things — as, apparently, one is aware of the first tremor of an earthquake. Since the Great War one had lived, in spite of minor pains and alarms, on the whole removed from danger. With this tremor of the crowd I was back in those days of the War again, a world of hourly expectation of death, a world no worse than the secure one, perhaps, but utterly different in all its rules and processes.

I remember that I instantly accepted this tremor as a portent. " One is not safe then after all. That danger may return." I was back in Petrograd watching from my high office window the revolutionaries firing down the street. " Trust no Russian ever," the old French journalist had said to me. " The mixture in them of East and West makes them unpredictable even to themselves." Well, but these were Italians and they were beginning to sway very unpleasantly indeed.

Policemen had been driving back the front rows, and the back rows were pressing forward. The women began to scream. The pressure grew more active. The great mass became rhythmical as though following music. A townsfellow behind

us began to shout as though demented: "Basta!
Basta!"

I had been in many many crowds and I knew
well that moment when one sets one's shoulders
and presses back with one's calves, laughing good-
humouredly, calling out to people to keep calm.
But, quite suddenly now, there was no good-
humour at all. People began to strike with their
hands. The huge monk with the beard turned
furiously to the man who was shouting "Basta!"
A woman began to cry that she was falling.

And then I felt myself lifted and knew that I
was carried off my feet. I was helpless and the
sense of that was so ominous to me that it was as
though I were about to be crushed to death.

"So this is the end of my Roman adventure!"
I thought.

I fancied that I had a last vision of Hilaire
Belloc, lifted up, transcended, in air, waving a
sandwich. I heard people call out "The steps!
The steps!" I saw Tom Driberg in his elegant
evening dress and white gloves, still smiling and
courteous although he seemed to be bent sideways.
"The steps! The steps!"

They were to the left of us, a whole flight of
them, and if at the top of them people fell there
would be a dreadful disaster to record in the

evening papers of the world. I was being carried as though a wind drove me, nearer and nearer to the steps, and I remember that I thought, " It's an omen. If we get safely over this there'll be no war."

I saw a woman disappear. A great wave hit us in the back. I saw Driberg's white gloves. I slid. I slipped. I slid. I was almost down. I was up again. I rushed, as though I were eagerly greeting a friend, to the outer wall. I stayed, breathless; my waistcoat was torn, my shoes trampled to pieces.

I looked to the balcony, but the ceremony was over.

I never saw Pope Pius XII crowned.

XIX

I SHOULD, perhaps, end there, for that truly was the end of my Adventure. Next morning I left Rome for Florence.

But it was not truly the end. I had, later, a final moment. Weary and cleaned, I did my piece for the Hearst papers (it was the worst of all my articles). We dined all of us together very late, and at length I walked up that old road, up that old hill, to my bed.

It was five minutes to midnight. In another five minutes I should be fifty-five and beginning my own private year of perilous, exciting, rewarding, disappointing experience.

I was breathless at that point opposite the flower-shop and the shoe-shop where I always stopped. Down the hill the broad curving street ran like a gleaming sheet of water. There was no one about. A moon, a little moon like a bird-pecked cherry, hung, stalkless, above the high roofs opposite me. The night air was scented with the merging of spring into very early summer, a warm rough scent of carnations and the new luxuriance of budding trees. After all, I had not found my Fountain. And I knew why. I was not yet worthy of it. When I had seen it before I had been a boy with a boy's simplicities. Now I carried a load of complexities, moral, mental and, especially, spiritual.

I sighed (a little perhaps because I was out of breath). I would return to Rome and search again, when I had become a wise, controlled, well-educated man. And then I would find it.

But I *had* found something. Four shadows, friendly and intimate, stood, marking with their grey austerity the waters of the road — the Poet whose physical life had been so brief, the Sculptor, that old wise man the Mountaineer who had been so simple a father to his many children, and the Saint beside whom I had stood for so brief a moment. Presumptuous to call them friends, but at least I had found them here and would never lose them again.

By them I would judge mankind. If such men could be thus, the soul of man was immortal and it was good to be joyful.

Jesus said unto him, Thou shalt love the Lord thy God with all thy heart, and with all thy soul, and with all thy mind. This is the first and great commandment. And the second is like unto it, Thou shalt love thy neighbour as thyself. On these two commandments hang all the Law and the Prophets.

It was no revelation that came to me. Something very much simpler. I knew that for myself this was the law of the world and the explanation of all things. I could not say what it would be for anyone else, and I was not at all blind as to how often I should myself fail in it — yes, again and again and again. But I knew an impulse of great happiness. Whatever might come, I had seen clearly what was the truth of things for me.

As I walked up the hill I heard a bell strike the hour. For myself a new year was already rushing along, eating up the minutes, and not a second to be lost!

THE END

Printed in Great Britain by R. & R. CLARK, LIMITED, *Edinburgh.*